THE ECONOMIST OF THE COUNTRY:
LUDWIG VON MISES IN THE
HISTORY OF MONETARY THOUGHT

THE ECONOMIST OF THE COUNTRY: LUDWIG VON MISES IN THE HISTORY OF MONETARY THOUGHT

by

James Rolph Edwards

A Hearthstone Book

Carlton Press, Inc.   New York, N.Y.

CONTENTS

1. Hypothesis, History and Methodology of the Austrian School 9
   Introduction: Purpose of the Study 9
   Hypothesis and Methodology of the Study 11
   The Contributions of the Austrian School 14
   A Synoptic Biography of Ludwig von Mises 16
   Methodology of Mises and the Older Austrians 20
   A Note on Editions and the Plan of the Study 24
2. The Nature, Development and Supply of Money 29
   Nominalism and the Classical Dichotomy 29
   The Functions and Origins of Money 31
   Value and Measurement 33
   Definitions and Components of the Money Stock 36
   Stock Demand Analysis 38
   Money as an Economic Good 41
3. The Regression Theorem and the Demand for Money . 49
   Introduction 49
   The Austrian Circle and the Regression Theorem 49
   Evaluation of Money and Demand: Objections 52
   Subjective Determinants of Real Balances Demanded 56
   Criticism and Defense of the Regression Theorem 57
   The Walrasian Solution to the Circularity Problem 58
   Mises and Patinkin: the Similarities 61
   Recurrence of the Circularity Problem 63
4. The Value of Money and Exchange Rates 69
   Introduction 69
   The Monetary Approach to International Adjustment 69
   Monetary Crises and the Development of the MAIA 72
   Mises and Purchasing-Power Parity 73
   The Balance of Payments and the Distribution of Money . 75
   Expectations and the Exchange Rate 78
   The Critique of the Balance of Payments Theory 82
   Mises and the Historians of the Monetary Approach 83

5. Inflation and Monetary Policy 91
   Introduction 91
   The Lagged Price Adjustment Mechanism 91
   The Social Consequences of Inflation 95
   Inflation, Real Wages and Unemployment 97
   The Nature and Adjustment of Inflationary Expectations . 100
   Inflation and the Demand for Money 104
   The Political Economy of Inflation 107
   Monetary Policy 109
6. Banking and the Business Cycle 117
   Introduction 117
   Banking, Credit and Fiduciary Media 117
   Money, Interest and the Wicksellian Doctrine 118
   The Austrian Theory of the Business Cycle 120
   The Fate of the Austrian Trade Cycle Theory 122
   Significance of the Austrian Theory 123
7. Summary and Conclusions 131
   Doctrinal Contributions of Mises' Monetary Writings 131
   Mises' Position in Doctrinal History 134

THE ECONOMIST OF THE COUNTRY: LUDWIG VON MISES IN THE HISTORY OF MONETARY THOUGHT

1
HYPOTHESIS, HISTORY AND METHODOLOGY
OF THE AUSTRIAN SCHOOL

Introduction: Purpose of the Study

The turn of the last century saw the publication of two works in monetary theory which have been recognized as classics: Knut Wicksell's *Interest and Prices* in 1889 and Irving Fisher's *Purchasing Power of Money* in 1911. The next recognized classic is Alfred Marshall's *Money, Credit and Commerce*, published in 1923, much of the material for which came from unpublished essays, written as early as the 1880s and from testimony Marshall had given before various parliamentary commissions over the years. In the 1930s monetary theory attained much of its essentially modern form, though it was not fully integrated with value theory until 1956, with the publication of Don Patinkin's *Money, Interest and Prices*.[1]

The latter task, among others, however, had been attempted in 1912 in a little-known classic entitled *Theorie des Geldes und der Umlaufsmittel*, published in German by an Austrian economist named Ludwig von Mises, and later translated as *The Theory of Money and Credit*. Mises and his work were influential on the continent, but never attained much status with American economists, except for his business-cycle theory, which became widely known due to its development in English by his most famous student, F.A. Hayek.[2] The relative obscurity of Mises' contributions to monetary theory may partly be due to the fact that *The Theory of Money and Credit* and certain of his other early works were unavailable in English translations for some decades following their initial publication.[3] By that time important contributions on many of the subjects he developed had been

9

published by other economists.

Of course, it is not the case that Mises' contributions have gone entirely unrecognized by western economists. In 1969 the American Economic Association names Mises a Distinguished Fellow and published the following citation:

> A library possessing all the books by Ludwig von Mises would have nineteen volumes if it confined itself to first editions, forty-six volumes if it included all revised editions and foreign translations, and still more if it possessed the Festschriften and other volumes, containing contributions by him. The stream of publications began in 1902. Mises will be 88 years old this September. He taught at the *Institut Universitaire* in Geneva until 1940. He still teaches at New York University. The stream of students that has come out of his seminars is no less remarkable than his literary output.
>
> His published work ranges from economic history and history of thought to methodology and political philosophy, with special emphasis on monetary theory, international finance, business fluctuations, price and wage theory, industrial organization, and economic systems. It would not be possible to enumerate the ideas which Mises has originated and disseminated over the years, but some of the most fruitful may be mentioned: in monetary theory, the application of marginal utility theory to the demand for money; in business cycle theory, certain amendments to the Wicksellian theory of the cumulative process and a demonstration that a monetary policy stabilizing certain price indices would not at the same time stabilize business activity; in the theory of socialist economic planning, the discovery that the type of economic calculation required for an efficient allocation of resources cannot be carried out without a system of competitive market prices. The recent movements toward decentralized planning in several Soviet type economies add the endorsement of history to the insights at which Mises arrived almost fifty years ago. [1]

Despite the almost effusive praise and recognition in this citation, the fact is that with regard to most of the ideas Mises developed in monetary theory of which western specialists are aware, their validity or significance as contributions is in dispute to say the least, and in most cases the judgement rendered on them has been negative. Mises' monetary business cycle theory, for example, which spawned a large literature in the twenties which extended into the forties, was firmly rejected and has been virtually forgotten, until just recently. With regard to the application of marginal analysis to the demand for money, Patinkin not only denied the validity of Mises' solution, but of the very problem it was based upon.[5]

To say that such judgments have been negative, however, is only to refer to a majority of academic specialists in a give field at a given time. In the social sciences significant viewpoints never entirely disappear. Mises represented such viewpoint, since he was not just an Austrian economist but a member of the Austrian School, which was and is a distinct subset of neoclassical thought. Recently, as part of an ongoing re-examination and criticism of the neoclassical paradigm from both internal and external sources, there has emerged a certain amount of interest in the Austrian approach and in Mises' work in particular.

Perhaps most of the interest in Mises has centered on his later contributions to the theory of entrepreneurship and the market process, but there has been at least one substantial and not entirely critical essay on his monetary theory.[6] It is the purpose of this study to do a more extensive analysis of Mises' monetary theory within the context of the history of monetary thought in order to establish just what his contributions were, if any. With the exception of a few general comments on the Austrian approach below, no other aspects of Mises' economics will be considered except where they relate to or are background for the development of his monetary theory.

Hypothesis and Methodology of the Study

Any attempt to assess the contributions of an economist such as Mises rests on implicit criteria for what constitutes a worthwhile contribution, and perhaps it is best to make them explicit at this point. The question of what constitutes a contribution has two levels, however. The first concerns what constitutes a contribution on the part of the economist under discussion. The second concerns how the historian of thought makes a contribution by pointing out or demonstrating the contributions of the economist under discussion.

In judging the subject economist's contributions, one might

11

have resort to the court of academic acceptance, and indeed any idea or theory which gives rise to a significant literature participated in by other economists must be judged a significant contribution, even where that idea is ultimately rejected. This is precisely what happened to Mises' theory of the business cycle. One problem with an acceptance criterion is this: acceptance often implies that the origin of the idea or theory is well-known, and the historian of thought makes no contribution in pointing out what everyone knows. It often happens, however, that implications of an idea are developed by others while its originator is forgotten, and in such cases the historian of thought makes a contribution in pointing out that origin.

A second problem with an acceptance criterion is that academicians can make mistakes, either in judging or failing to see important implications of an idea or theory. The historian of thought is himself an analyst and has a perfect right to judge such an idea or theory as significant, and can assert such significance if he can provide the logical or empirical basis for his conclusion. In such a case, of course, the judgment whether the historian of thought has himself made a contribution rests with others.

Originality may seem to be a criterion for a significant contribution, and it is usually important and implicit in other criteria, such as those mentioned above. Originality is not sufficient, however, for many original ideas are either incorrect or trivial. Neither is it necessary, except in an oblique sense. It is often a contribution to simply *rejuvenate* a significant idea or theory where such rejuvenation is successful and the idea or theory again becomes significant in the literature. One of Mises' most important contributions, the purchasing-power-parity doctrine, was precisely of this nature, and oddly enough his role in the matter was largely forgotten until just recently.

There is another way in which originality may play only an oblique part. It can be a significant contribution simply to produce a synthesis of existing ideas even if no other original contribution is made, where such a synthesis results in a more extensive and coherent unity than previously existed. In many respects Mises was just such a synthesizer, though he always made at least marginal contributions in the process. Indeed, the central characteristic of Mises as a theorist was that he was a system builder.

It should also be pointed out that precursors make contributions even if their ideas are rejected in their day and those ideas are rediscovered, developed and accepted later on a completely independent basis. Dupuit and Gossen deserve less credit than Menger, Jevons and Walras in the history of marginal utility theory, but only for their failure in convincing others, not for any lack of originality and logical significance of their contributions. And last, it is sometimes a significant contribution simply to ask the right questions, even where the answers given are not satisfactory, if others are not even dealing with them at the time. The historian of thought makes his contribution by demonstrating such contributions on the part of the individual or individuals under discussion.

The analysis of Mises' monetary theory will begin in the next chapter. The hypothesis to be tested by analysis, documentary evidence, and reference to the criteria discussed is that Mises made no contributions worthy of note to monetary theory and related topics which have not already been recognized by orthodox western economists and credited in their histories of monetary thought or general doctrinal histories. The empirical element of the study will be the contents of Mises' early monetary writings and of the doctrinal histories mentioned.[7] The hypothesis will be shown to be false.

While this approach will be followed throughout the study, it should be briefly moderated in one respect. Men make history, have ideas, and create systems of thought, but it is also true that ideas, viewpoints and historical conditions affect men.[8] It is far too easy to judge a historical-intellectual figure by the standards of a later period. Objective assessment of such an individual requires some sensitivity to his unique conditions and viewpoint. As an "Austrian" economist, Mises should be seen in his intellectual and historical context, so some discussion of the Austrian School and of Mises' life and times is in order. This task will be undertaken in the next three sections.

Among the erroneous notions current in the history of economic doctrines is the view that the marginal revolution was a consequence of the development of calculus.[9] This view ignores the mathematical sophistication of Gossen and Depuit, who failed to start the revolution, and the strong possibility that the revolution would not have been successful without the Austrians, among whose central methodological peculiarities was a militant rejection of mathematics either in analysis or exposition. The originator of the Austrian School was Carl Menger.

Menger (1840-1921) was born in Galicia, Austria. He studied law at the University of Vienna and in Prague, later finishing his doctorate at the University of Cracow in 1867. In 1871 he published his *Grundsätze der Volkswirthshaftslehre* (later translated as *Principles of Economics*). He was appointed Extraordinary Professor at Vienna in 1873, where he taught until he retired in 1903. The *Grundsätze* was a masterpiece of insight, clarity and systematic exposition. Starting with a discussion of causality and the means-end relation, Menger first discussed useful objects, then goods, then scarce or economic goods.

Without a mathematical symbol, Menger derived both diminishing marginal utility and the equimarginal principle. The first was not explained in terms of a continuous tendency toward satiation, as in Jevons or Walras. In fact, utility was not a sensory or hedonistic unit at all. The utility of the marginal unit was simply the importance to the individual of the end which could no longer be obtained when a unit of a supply was lost. So the importance of marginal units declined as supply increased simply because additional units were always applied to the most important remaining unsatisfied use, and hence to progressively less important uses *ceteris paribus*.[10]

This approach is much more congenial to an ordinal view of utility than the "hedonistic calculus" of Jevons and Walras, but Menger confused the issue by using cardinal numbers in his arithmetic examples. His early followers followed him in his error here, but Mises, as we shall see in the next chapter, developed this approach into a fully ordinal value theory.

In analytically deriving value from the means-ends relation, and in arguing that the anticipated value to be obtained determined the costs to be expended, not vice-versa, Menger realized that he was reversing previous value theory. And that the chief difficulty he would face would be in explaining the imputation of the value of economic goods to their factors of production. To do so he distinguished between first-order goods, or goods valued for their direct use, and higher-order goods, or goods valued only for their usefulness in producing lower (ultimately first) order goods. He conceived of production as taking time and as taking place in stages, in each of which decision makers anticipated the quantities demanded and prices offered at the next stage. In many passages Menger discussed complementarity and substitutability among inputs and elaborated the essentials of the marginal productivity theory of factor valuation.[11]

Menger's book seems to have had no impact on opinion in the economics profession for several years. It was not until the mid 1880s that two students of Menger's, Eugen von Böhm-Bawerk (1851-1914) and Friedrich von Wieser (1851-1926) began developing his insights and actively promoting the new paradigm. Frustration at this lack of response and anger at an unfavorable review of his book by Gustav Schmoller led Menger into a long and bitter debate on methodology with the Younger (German) Historical School. This debate has since been labeled the *methodenstreit,* or struggle over method.

Menger never denied the usefulness of historical studies within their purview. What he opposed was the attempt to arrive at laws of historical development of economic institutions by historical studies. In his view social aggregates (of which economic examples include such concepts as market demand and supply, the price level, national income, etc.) were to be reconstructed analytically from their units.[12] We now call this methodological individualism. Menger based his methodology on the essentialist view of Aristotelian metaphysics, which involved seeking the essence of economic relationships in terms of those elements which must always be present by virtue of the nature of the relationships. From these he felt economic laws could be discovered which would not be relative to time and place.[13]

Though Menger may have felt neglected, he was actually more

15

successful at attracting adherents of high caliber than Jevons or Walras were. Böhm-Bawerk, for example, besides being an economic theorist and professor at the University of Vienna, was also an extremely capable public servant. He was the Austrian Minister of Finance three times and participated in the introduction of the gold standard and the removal of the Austrian sugar subsidy.[14]

Böhm-Bawerk's most famous work was *Kapital und Kapitalizins* (translated as *Capital and Interest*), published in three volumes between 1884 and 1912. The first volume was a critique of previous interest theories. In his second volume he developed many of Menger's ideas on production into his famous theory of capital and interest. The theory centered on the role of capital in extending the period and efficiency of production and on the role of subjective time preferences in accounting for the phenomenon of interest through the valuation of intermediate goods at different stages in the production process.

Friedrich von Wieser, the other important student of Menger, was the son of a government official and later Böhm-Bawerk's brother-in-law. Wieser also studied for two years in German universities under the Historical economists Karl Knies, William Roscher and Bruno Hildebrand. During Knies' seminar Wieser developed the concept of opportunity cost.[15] His most developed exposition of this quintessentially subjectivist and "Austrian" doctrine came with the publication of *Der Natürliche Werth* in 1889 (translated as *Natural Value*). When Menger retired Wieser obtained his chair at the University of Vienna. Later Wieser became an Austrian MP and Minister of Commerce.[16] Thus, he and Böhm-Bawerk not only gave the Austrian School a tradition of theoretical excellence, but of practical policy application. As we shall see, Mises carried on both of these traditions.

A Synoptic Biography of
Ludwig von Mises

Much of the information available on Mises' life up to 1940 comes from an autobiography he compiled in that year which was not published until 1978, six years after his death.[17] He was born in 1881 in Lemburg, Austria, now the city of Lvov,

U.S.S.R., and entered the Uiversity of Vienna in 1900.[18] At that time, he claims to have been a "thorough statist" though a prolonged reading of Marxist and historicist literature had led him to reject both of those variants of statism.[19]

At first, Mises studied law and economic history, but a reading of Menger's *Grundsätze* in 1903 converted him to a lifetime study of economics. Mises also read Karl Helfferich's book on monetary theory (*Das Geld*, 1903) at this time, in which Helfferich denied the applicability of Austrian value theory to the demand for money. It was apparently this conjunction which motivated Mises to undertake *The Theory of Money and Credit*. Shortly after reading Menger's book, Mises began attending Böhm-Bawerk's seminar and continued until 1913.[20]

In 1908, Mises joined the Central Association for Housing Reform, and after observing certain detrimental affects of government intervention in housing he experienced another conversion, this time to the normative views of 19th century liberalism.[21] The next year, he obtained employment with the Austrian Chamber of Commerce. The Chamber was a semi-official body, originally formed some decades before by businessmen, but financed by a tax. By this time, the Chamber had become an influential adviser to the government.

Mises gained his appointment at the recommendation of an economist, named Victor Graetz, who was leaving the Chamber, and Mises made his living in that position until 1934. Mises would have preferred to work solely as a teacher. He did become a lecturer in economics at the University of Vienna in 1913, but he was never promoted past the level of Associate Professor,[22] though he was named Extraordinary Professor.[23] Mises blamed this on prejudice against his liberal views.

At any rate, Mises may have had more influence on national events in his position with the Chamber than if he had become a pure academician. His reputation on the continent was assured with the publication of *The Theory of Money and Credit*, and though nominally he was just an employee of the Chamber he became, in his own words, "the economist of the country," whose advice was sought (though also by his own admission, seldom taken) by the leaders of all Austrian political parties.[24]

Mises was an Austrian patriot and an opponent of all forms of statism in a time and place where neither of those attitudes was fashionable. Around the turn of the century, Mises writes, the continued existence of Austria as a nation was in doubt. The state did not overlap with linguistic lines, and according to Mises the majority of its citizens neither wanted it to continue as an independent nation nor believed it could.[25]

Austria was also beset by factional and political strife. The three major political parties were the Christian Social, The German National, and the Social Democratic. The last of these was a Marxist party, acording to Mises, and had its own paramilitary force from 1905 on. Apparently the allies allowed the Social Democrats access to Austrian military arms at the end of World War I, and Mises says that by 1923 the "proletarian" army was much larger than the combined Austrian military and police. Begining in the winter of 1918-19 other groups attempted to form countervailing paramilitary organizations.[26]

The winter of 1918-19 was, consequently, a crisis point. In what is certainly the most astounding assertion in Mises' partial autobiography, he claims to have sat up for three nights running with Otto Bauer, the leader of the Social Democratic party, and talked him out of leading a communist takeover of Austria, primarily on the basis that Austria was dependent on food imports, hence the Allies could have starved out a Marxist Austrian state in short order.[27] It seems unlikely that independent confirmation of this occurrence can be obtained now, but if it is true it is an indication of Mises' importance in post World War I Austria.

Apparently as a result of such experiences Mises decided to attempt to destroy the intellectual respectability of socialism. The result was the publication in 1922 of a book later translated as *Socialism*.[28] Its central argument may be the one idea Mises is best known for: that it is impossible to allocate resources efficiently in a socialist state due to the absence of a market, and hence of market prices, for the factors of production. This argument and its implications resulted in a debate in journals and books which lasted for over twenty years.[29] Indeed, Mises' fame, or rather infamy on this point and on his methodological views (see below), may have over-shadowed his early contributions in monetary theory.

Following the war, Austria engaged in a policy of inflation on the same order as that of Germany, and Mises bent all of his energies to getting it stopped. The efforts he made, along with a few allies such as Graetz and Wilhelm Rosenburg, were probably aided by the fact that he had extensively analyzed the subject in his 1912 book, to the point that that work may have seemed virtually prophetic. In 1922, he and his supporters succeeded in convincing the leaders of the Christian Social Party, who were then in power, to stop the monetary expansion. The value of the Austrian monetary unit, the Crown, was stabilized. The government began inflating again after 1931 when a large Austrian bank, the Kreditanstalt, collapsed, but Mises again succeeded in getting it stopped. It is clear from his autobiography, however, that among the internal political division, the pressures for monetary expansion, and the rise of totalitarianism in Germany, Mises felt he was fighting a losing battle and was becoming somewhat discouraged at this time.[30]

Mises' greatest sense of satisfaction and accomplishment in this period probably came from a private seminar which he began in 1920 and continued until he left Vienna. Indeed, this seminar has added greatly to Mises' reputation. It was held once every two weeks from October to June in his office at the Chamber, and attracted many students who became notable scholars. Among the regular attenders were Gottfried Haberler, F. A. Hayek, Fritz Machlup, Oskar Morgenstern, Alfred Schutz, Richard von Stigl, Erich Voegelin and many others who attained international reputations.[31] Mises was so proud of his seminar that he wrote "...in this circle the Viennese culture produced one of its last blossoms...."[32]

In 1934, Mises was offered the position of Professor of International Economic Relations at the Graduate Institute of International Studies in Geneva and he accepted immediately. Mises enjoyed his position at the Institute a great deal. Not only was it an excellent teaching position, but the intellectual atmosphere at the Institute was compatible with his 19th century liberal views. Under other circumstances he would have remained there but by 1940, as a prominent anti-totalitarian Austrian refugee, Mises felt himself to be something of an embarrassment and threat to the neutral Swiss government, so he left for the United States.[33]

From 1945 until near the end of his life, Mises taught as an unsalaried Visiting Professor at New York University, Graduate School of Business Administration, supported by the William Volker Fund and earnings from his publications.[34] During this period, Mises wrote many of his better-known works, including his magnum opus, *Human Action*, which integrated his entire economic and methodological system.[35] Also, he was not without outstanding students and converts in this period, such as Henry Hazlitt, Leonard Read, Murray Rothbard, George Reisman, and William Burdick.

There are those who would claim that Mises had a profound effect on American conservative thought.[36] Certainly the list of conservative and libertarian thinkers who admit such influence is large.[37] *Human Action* has been prominent in conservative booklists almost continuously since its first publication, and some of his other books have circulated widely. Mises seldom published in English-language economic journals, however, and thus his contributions remain, at this date, somewhat obscure to professional economists.[38] He died in 1972 at the age of 91.

Methodology of Mises and the Older Austrians

While it may have been the similarities in the views of Jevons, Walras, and Menger and his followers which most struck the economic world, there were also important differences, the most obvious being that Jevons and Walras expressed their views mathematically, while the Austrians did not. This has often been criticized as a methodological fault. Stigler, for example, wrote that the problem with Jevons was that he did not know enough mathematics, and with the Austrians that they knew none at all.[39]

Now it may (or may not) be true that little training in mathematics led the early Austrians to a predilection against a mathematical approach and that their explicit arguments against the use of mathematics were largely rationalizations. If we place any credence in their own statements, however, the real reason they avoided mathematics was their unwillingness to abstract from what *they* considered essential properties of the subject matter under consideration. In their view, by the very nature of simultaneous equations, time, causality, and process are absent; simultaneous equations do not explain but only describe, and they describe only equilibria. Since the Austrians were centrally concerned with explaining temporal economic processes, they thought that a method which was explicitly subjectivist and causal-genetic rather than functional (in the sense of modeling with simultaneous equations) was superior.[40]

Carl Menger's son, also named Carl Menger, became an eminent mathematician, and did important work in mathematical economics in the 1930s. Yet, recently, the younger Menger discussed and defended the Austrian aversion to mathematical economics, pointing out some of its limitations. Even in the physical sciences, he argued, mathematics is not a method of research so much as a mode of expression and description. Mathematics cannot originate statements about the universe, but only produce transformations of such statements put in mathematical form. Such transformations are useful and illuminating at times, but all such statements and transformations are preceded by logical, causal inquiry.

> The road from the blow of the hammer of an irate god to the disturbance of the air caused (*sit venia verbo!*) by an immense electric spark, is not paved with the discoveries of functional relations....[41]

The Austrian interest in explaining choice in terms of particular units led them to reject calculus, since calculus abstracts from the lumpiness of the real world. Instead of using smooth, continuous and differentiable utility functions, in which infinitesimal changes in quantities yield infinitesimal changes in satisfaction (a view with inherently hedonistic overtones), the Austrians always assumed discontinuous relations in which discrete units of means were applied to the attainment of particular ends. The contrast in results is illuminating. Price determination arrived at by the functional approach is absolutely precise. Prices arrived at by the Austrian approach are set only within zones of indeterminacy, bounded by the subjective valuations of the marginal buyers and sellers.[42]

Of course, the real world is one of discrete units, temporal sequence and disequilibrium. It is necessary, however, to abstract from the world in the creation of any economic model. The

Austrians never disagreed with this. Their question is: Are discrete units, temporal sequence and disequilibrium extraneous elements, to be pared away in the process of abstraction, or should they be the central focus?

The Austrians answered that those elements *are* the reality to be studied, and they must be studied in a particular way because they have a peculiar character or motivation which is subjective more than physical. Discreteness is a matter of human definition or purpose. Time is peculiarly subjective, and the human view of temporal distance is subject to a perspective similar to that inherent in the observation of spatial distance. Causality also has a peculiar character in human phenomena, being teleological rather than mechanical. Most disequilibrating and all equilibrating forces in economic processes are subjective in origin. All economic processes are the result of human action and interactions as people try to adjust themselves to changing conditions and attain subjective ends.[43]

Now all of this must sound strange to orthodox economists. For one thing, it clashes with the dominant positivist methodology. Positivism asserts that no statement that is not susceptible to empirical falsification can be considered meaningful. The way to economic knowledge then (or at least a knowledge of what is *not* true), is to confront hypotheses with the evidence. On that basis, as Milton Friedman has stressed, the realism of the assumptions is meaningless, and only predictability counts.[44] To the Austrians, on the other hand, the realism of the assumptions is clearly central.

Second, Austrians sometimes seem intent on differentiating their product to the point of ignoring major points of overlap between Austrian and orthodox methods. There is a strong strain of subjectivism in orthodox neoclassical analysis, which has in fact assimilated such Austrian notions as opportunity costs and time preference, along with vital Walrasian and Marshallian contributions. The Austrians may also overstress the problems with mathematical methods, which *can* be applied in discrete analysis, and *can* incorporate time as a variable, if somewhat inadequately.[45]

The point here, though, is not to agree or disagree with the Austrian style of analysis so much as to understand it as a paradigm which Mises assimilated, applied and developed. Menger's stage theory of production and Böhm-Bawerk's capital theory became central to his monetary theory of the business cycle. Time entered explicitly into his theory of the demand for money, as we shall see. Menger's essentialism became the essence of Mises' methodology, which he called praxeology. This consisted of a set of ontological axioms such as scarcity, uncertainty, causality and positive time preference which Mises saw in Kantian fashion as literal categories of perception from which the corpus of economics was to be deduced *a priori*. In theory, if the axioms were *axioms* (not just arbitrary postulates), and the deductions were performed correctly, the resulting theorems had the same truth status and were not subject to empirical falsification.[46]

Such a view made Mises an adamant opponent of positivism. He thought economic events were too complex and unique for empirical methods based on any frequency interpretation of probability to be capable of discovering economic laws.[47]

> The impracticability of measurements is not due to the lack of technical methods for the establishment of measure. It is due to the absence of constant relations. If it were only caused by technical insufficiency, at least an approximate estimation would be possible in some cases. But the main fact is that there are no constant relations. Economics is not, as ignorant positivists repeat again and again, backward because it is not "quantitative." It is not quantitative and does not measure because there are no constants. Statistical figures referring to economic events are historical data. They tell us what happened in a nonrepeatable historical case. Physical events can be interpreted on the ground of our knowledge concerning constant relations established by experiments. Historical events are not open to such an interpretation.[48]

Propagation of this view in numerous works beginning in the 1920s left Mises estranged from western economists who were increasingly wedded to the notion that only testable propositions are meaningful. This was true despite the fact that Karl Popper, who was more responsible than anyone else for the advance of that notion, was well aware of the limitations of such an approach in economics.

In physics,....the parameters of our equations can, in principle, be reduced to a small number of constants, a reduction which has been successfully carried out in a number of cases. This is not so in economics; here the parameters are themselves, in the most important cases, quickly changing variables. This clearly reduces the significance, interpretability, and testability of our measurements.[49]

Of course Mises' explicit writings on methodology followed the early writings on monetary theory with which this essay is concerned, but from the first he essentially practiced what he later preached.

A Note on Editions and the Plan of the Study

The only translation of Mises' *Theorie des Geldes und der Umlaufsmittel* (*The Theory of Money and Credit*) was made by H. E. Batson. Subsequent editions are all of this translation. The edition used by Batson was the second, 1924 German Edition, which Mises had revised. At least some of the obscurity regarding what Mises did and when he did it is due to this fact, even though he discussed some of the changes in his prefaces to later editions. In the present study, in order to leave no doubt regarding the presence of certain ideas and arguments in the original edition, footnote references will often be made to that edition, a copy of which was obtained for this purpose. Such references to the 1912 edition will be supplementary, of course, to references to a recent edition of the English translation.

The present study will largely follow the order of topics covered in *The Theory of Money and Credit* itself, deleting those judged less significant and focusing on those judged more crucial. Chapter 2 will deal with Mises' discussion of the nature of money and the money supply, as well as with a preliminary correction he made in value theory which is of some doctrinal importance. Chapter 3, perhaps the heart of the study, deals with Mises' theory of the demand for money and the determination of the value of money, along with certain controversies that resulted.

Chapter 4 will discuss Mises' contributions to the monetary theories of the balance of payments and exchange rate determination. Chapter 5 covers his theory of the inflationary process and the political economy of inflation, as well as his conclusions regarding monetary policy. Chapter 6 covers Mises' views of banking and the business cycle, and chapter 7 will summarize the results obtained in the preceding chapters.

[1] Patinkin himself believes this to be one of the accomplishments of Keynes in *The General Theory*, though Patinkin remarks that Keynes was "not completely successful in this respect." See Don Patinkin, *Anticipations of the General Theory?* (Chicago: University of Chicago Press, 1982): 13.

[2] See chapter 6 for discussion and citations.

[3] For example, Mises' 1912 work was not published in English until 1934. For other examples, see chapter 4 below.

[4] "Ludwig von Mises, Distinguished Fellow, 1969," *American Economic Review* 49 (September 1969): Frontispiece.

[5] Don Patinkin, *Money, Interest and Prices*, 2d ed. (New York: Harper and Row, 1965): 115-116. See also chapter 3 below.

[6] Larence S. Moss, "The Monetary Economics of Ludwig von Mises," in Lawrence S. Moss, ed., *The Economics of Ludwig von Mises* (Kansas City: Sheed and Ward, 1976): 13-49. On recent developments of the Misesian concept of competition and the market process see Israel Kirzner, *Competition and Entrepreneurship* (Chicago: University of Chicago Press, 1974), W. Duncan Reekie, *Industry, Prices and Markets* (New York: Halsted Press, 1979): especially the introduction and chapter 6, and S.C. Littlechild and G. Owen, "An Austrian Model of the Entrepreneurial Market Process," *Journal of Economic Theory* 23 (December 1980): 361-379.

[7] Patinkin has pointed out that the history of doctrines should be regarded as an empirical science in the sense that economists can and should support their interpretations with evidence from the texts. He further argues that doctrinal researchers attempting to ascertain the *central* message of an economist's work are much like econometricians trying to fit a regression line to a set of empirical observations. *Anticipations of the General Theory?*: 16-17.

[8] I am *not* here arguing for *any* variation of the Marxist theory of ideology or the sociology of knowledge. As I have argued elsewhere, in specific denial of those viewpoints, such contextual elements simply enter as inputs, along with volitional mental labor, into the mental production process of the individual. See James Rolph Edwards, "Ideology, Economics and Knowledge," *Reason Papers* No. 7 (Spring 1981): 53-71.

[9] Maurice Dobb, *Theories of Value and Distribution Since Adam Smith* (Cambridge: Cambridge University Press, 1973): 168.

[10] F. A. Hayek, "The Place of Menger's Grundsätze in the History of Economic

Thought," in J.R. Hicks and W. Weber, eds., *Carl Menger and the Austrian School of Economics* (Oxford: Oxford University Press, 1973): 7.

[11]Carl Menger, *Principles of Economics* (Illinois: The Free Press, 1950): 149-152 and 162-165.

[12]*International Encyclopedia of the Social Sciences* 10 (1968): 125, hereafter cited as *IESS*.

[13]Leland Yeager, "The Methodology of Henry George and Carl Menger," *American Journal of Economics and Sociology* 13 (April 1954): 233-238.

[14]*IESS* 10: 125.

[15]*IESS* 16: 549.

[16]Ibid., 549.

[17]Ludwig von Mises, *Notes and Recollections* (South Holland, Illinois: Libertarian Press, 1978).

[18]Lawrence S. Moss, "Introduction," *The Economics of Ludwig von Mises*: 1.

[19]*Notes and Recollections*: 1-16.

[20]Ibid., 40-43.

[21]Ibid., 19-21.

[22]Ibid., 71-73 and 93-95.

[23]The title of "Extraordinary Professor" (actually "Professor Extraordinary" in the German) was thus honorary. Bettine Bien calls it a title. See Bettine Bien, *The Works of Ludwig von Mises* (New York: Foundation for Economic Education, 1970): 7. (This useful booklet is primarily a list of all of Mises' publications, in German, English and other languages.)

[24]*Notes and Recollections*: 71-74.

[25]Ibid., 27.

[26]Ibid., 88-90.

[27]Ibid., 77.

[28]Ludwig von Mises *Die Gemeinwirtschaft: Untersuchugen Uber den Socialismus* (Jena: Gustav Fischer, 1922).

[29]Hayek collected many of the most important essays from this debate in F.A. Hayek, ed., *Collectivist Economic Planning* (London: George Routledge and Sons, 1935) and published a later essay in his *Individualism and Economic Order* (Chicago: University of Chicago Press, 1948). See also A.P. Lerner, "Economic Theory and Socialist Economy," *Review of Economic Studies* 2 (October 1934): 51-61, T.E. Gregory, "An Economist Looks at Planning," *Manchester School of Economic and Social Studies* 4 No. 1 (1933): 1-14, H.D. Dinkinson, "Freedom and Planning: A reply to Dr. Gregory," *Manchester School of Economic and Social Studies* 4 No. 2 (1933): 82-89, T.J.B. Hoff, *Economic Calculation in the Socialist Society* (London: William Hodge and Co., 1949), and James Buchanan, *Cost and Choice* (Chicago: Markaham Co., 1969).

[30]*Notes and Recollections*: 77-83.

[31]Ibid., 97-100.

[32]Ibid., 77.

[33]Ibid., 136-138.

[34]Hans F. Sennholz, "Postscript," *Notes and Recollections*: 155.

[35]Ludwig von Mises, *Human Action*, 3rd ed. (Chicago: Henry Regnery Co., 1963).

[36]See John P. East, "American Conservative Thought: The Impact of Ludwig von

Mises," *Modern Age* 23 (Fall 1979): 338-339.

[37]See *Toward Liberty: Essays in Honor of Ludwig von Mises on the Occasion of his 90th Birthday*, Vol. 1 and II (Menlo Park: Institute for Humane Studies, 1971). A few of these authors did not meet Mises personally, but all admitted he influenced them.

[38]*The Works of Ludwig von Mises*: 25-37 lists all of Mises' articles published between 1940 and 1969, when he stopped publishing. Only two are in professional, English language, economic journals. One was a book review published in *The American Economic Review* in 1943. The other was a short essay on expectations and the business cycle published in *Economica* that same year, actually just a comment on an article by Ludwig Lachman in the previous issue. Mises did publish many articles in non-economic intellectual and academic journals in this period, however, but his prime efforts in economic theory went into his books.

[39]George J. Stigler, *Production and Distribution Theories* (New York: Macmillan, 1946): 181. See also Joseph Schumpeter's comments in his *History of Economic Analysis*, 4th ed. (New York: Oxford University Press, 1961): 954-956.

[40]See the quotation from a letter by Menger to Walras in T. W. Hutchinson, "Some Themes from Investigations into Method," *Carl Menger and The Austrian School of Economics*: 16.

[41]Carl Menger, "Austrian Marginalism and Mathematical Economics," Ibid., 54.

[42]See Eugen Böhm-Bawerk, *Value and Price* (An extract from *The Positive Theory of Capital*) (South Holland, Illinois: Libertarian Press, 1971): 117-130.

[43]The Austrians trace this viewpoint back to J.E. Cairnes and Nassau Senior, among others. See Murray N. Rothbard, "Praxeology: the Methodology of Austrian Economics," in Edwin G. Dolan, ed., *The Foundation of Modern Austrian Economics* (Kansas City: Sheed and Ward, 1976): 19-39, and Marian Bowley, *Nassau Senior and Classical Economics* (New York: Augustus M. Kelley, 1949): 27-65.

[44]See Milton Friedman, "The Methodology of Positive Economics," in *Essays in Positive Economics* (Chicago: University of Chicago Press, 1953): 3-43.

[45]See L. A. Boland, "Time in Economics vs Economics in Time: The Hayek Problem," *Canadian Journal of Economics* 11 (May 1978): 242-249.

[46]*Human Action*: 32-41.

[47]Mises based much of his view here on a distinction between "class probability" (frequency) and "case probability," which referred to unique events some of the determinants of which were not known. He felt that economic events fell in the latter category. See *Human Action*: 107-115. Oddly enough, this distinction is actually attributable to his brother, Richard von Mises, the eminent mathematician and statistician, who was responsible for the frequency interpretation of probability and was a prominent positivist. See *IESS* 16: 382-384.

[48]*Human Action*: 56

[49]Karl Popper, *The Poverty of Historicism* (London: Routledge and Kegan Paul, 1957): 143.

2
THE NATURE, DEVELOPMENT
AND SUPPLY OF MONEY

Introduction

In writing the *Theorie des Geldes und der Umlaufsmittal* (*The Theory of Money and Credit*), Mises intended an extensive reformulation and restatement of monetary theory. No careful reader can fail to be impressed with the scope, completeness and unity of the work. This chapter will focus on several of the preliminary concepts Mises felt impelled to clarify before approaching the heart of his subject: the theory of value, the origin of money and components of its stock, the treatment of the supply of and demand for money in stock terms, and the nature of money as an economic good. It may aid understanding, however, to begin with a few comments and a hypothesis on the state of monetary theory as Mises found it at the turn of the century.

Nominalism and the Classical
Dichotomy

The period in which Mises began his career might accurately be characterized as a transition period both for monetary systems and institutions on the one hand and monetary theory on the other. As regards the former, the character of entities used as money was changing as monetary systems shifted (one cannot say "evolved" due to the term's normative implications) away from commodity monies toward pure fiat monies, with checking-account entries, lacking any tangible existence, looming larger in importance.

Monetary theory cannot remain stable in the face of such institutional alteration, unless it is sufficiently advanced that it can already comprehend and explain the emerging institutions. Such was hardly the case. Indeed, at the time (even more so than now) monetary theorists were confused on such fundamentals as the nature of money, the components of its stock, the demand for money, and the determination of its value. The central expression of these confusions was the classical dichotomy: the value of money was supposedly determined by its supply or "quantity" alone, while the values of goods were determined catalytically by the interaction of supply and demand schedules, analytically derived in subjective neoclassical terms of marginal utility and opportunity costs.

The most crucial failure of all here was the failure successfully to apply marginal analysis to the demand for money, carefully to derive individual demand schedules and to aggregate up to the market demand. It was, indeed, widely accepted that it was impossible to do so, for reasons which will be discussed in detail in the next chapter.[1] An important consequence of this is that monetary analysis, particularly on the continent, was shunted into highly abstract debates on the metaphysical nature of money, and away from rigorous attempts to define its supply and demand and explain the determination of its value.

The prime expression of this metaphysical monetary theorizing was Nominalism. In the Nominalist view there were only two types of monetary theorists, the other being Metalists, who allegedly believed money to be a commodity possessing intrinsic value, and paper substitutes to be completely dependent for their value on the money commodity.[2] Nominalists denigrated this view as a "materialist conception." In their view money was a purely abstract conceptual entity, a pure number, essentially a unit of account.[3]

The preeminence of the abstract unit of account as the essence of money in Nominalist theory, in combination with the fact that Nominalists were universally quantity theorists with rather strong neutrality views, apparently justified spending little effort to solve the problem of the value of the medium of exchange. To be fair, some Nominalists, particularly a later group which Howard Ellis termed "Materialist Nominalists," who identified

30

the "ideal unit" more closely with the physical medium of exchange, did make some effort to discuss the determination of the letter's purchasing power. In explaining the demand for money, however, they never got beyond the vacuous, circular assertion that everyone demands it because everyone else does.[4]

It is an odd fact that the quantity theory has been accepted and used at different times both by advocates and opponents of inflation. A good example of its use by explicit inflationists is the Greenback and Free Silver movements in the 19th century United States.[5] It would probably not be fair to label all Nominalists as inflationists, but the propagation of Nominalism certainly weakened intellectual and popular support for a gold standard or any other institutional constraint on monetary expansion, and the effects of that on Germany in the 1920s is clear. That the connection is explicit is made clearer by the fact that Nominalism in the 20th century gained much of its impetus from G. F. Knapp's *State Theory of Money.*[6]

According to knapp, what was used as money in a given country was determined by the state by simply designating whatever it wanted to be legal tender. Though he argued that the state gives "value" to money by making it legal tender and agreeing to accept it, a charitable interpretation of this is that demand was thereby created, since he distinguished the exchange value or purchasing power of money as a separate problem and admitted that it was determined in exchange.[7] In other words, what the state determined was the choice of money, and it did so by mere legal act.

The Functions and Origins of Money

In contrast to the Nominalist view, from Menger[8] to Hayek,[9] a central element of Austrian economic theory has been an assertion that markets and economic institutions emerge spontaneously, and, like language and culture, are not planned creations. Menger specifically analyzed money in these terms, and early in *The Theory of Money and Credit* Mises explained and extended Menger's analysis of the spontaneous emergence of money.

Indirect exchange, Mises argued, becomes necessary as the division of labor extends and people's tastes become more refined.

31

He did not use the phrase "double coincidence of wants" that is so widely used now, but he was clearly discussing the same phenomena when he argued that not all goods are equally marketable (that is, as widely desired and accepted in as many markets), that those bringing highly marketable goods to market have a greater chance of success, and that because of this many such goods are adopted as media of exchange.[10]

When this occurs the marketability of such goods increases even more, increasing their demand and relative value,[11] and there then follows a long historical process of competition and selection among such media until only a few, primarily the precious metals, dominate. With lucid insight Mises pointed out that the motive of this process is the costliness of exchange transactions under a regime of multiple monies.[12] An explicit corollary to this whole view, which contrasts sharply with Nominalism, was that all the other functions of money (store of value, unit of account, etc.) rest on and derive from its use as a general medium of exchange.[13]

From the background of the "spontaneous origin" view Mises was bound to oppose a view such as Knapp's. Mises did not deny that the state was often the ultimate arbiter of the means of debt settlement within its boundaries, but he did deny that the choice was arbitrary. In his view the state could only choose from a set of exchange media the elements of which were determined in exchange, and if in so doing the state caused redistributions between creditors and debtors market actions such as gold clauses might emerge to offset the state action.[14]

Mises argued that the position of the state in regard to money was no different from that of any other party, except in the magnitude of its ability to affect demand and supply due to its enormous resources outside the market.[15] Merely passing a law requiring debts and taxes to be paid in a new medium was not sufficient, in his view, to effect a change in the monetary standard. Such a law could only be effective when the change had in fact been effected by economic means. The state first had to supply the new money and withdraw the old. He went on to point out that this inability of the state to determine the medium of exchange by purely legal action was illustrated by the historical operation of Gresham's law in frustrating state actions designed to integrate disparate metals into a uniform monetary system by fixing exchange rates between them.[16]

Reviewing these arguments, Ellis objected that it was an exaggeration for Mises to say that the position of the state regarding money was no different from that of other parties to the market, and that it could merely influence the choice of money, yet in essence he conceded Mises' point.[17] Nominalists writing after *The theory of Money and Credit* also seem to have conceded the point. Nussbaum, for example, cited his own examples of the operation of Gresham's law and of extra-governmental monies.[18]

Value and Measurement

While he thought it important to refute economic error, Mises' main intent in writing *The Theory of Money and Credit* was to clarify the foundations of monetary theory and steer it away from the esoteric metaphysical debates of Nominalism by solving the central problem: that is, by integrating monetary theory and value theory and eliminating the classical dichotomy.[19] Before he could do so, however, he felt that it was necessary to make a correction in value theory itself. In doing so, he made a contribution which has gone virtually unrecognized.

Mises' theory originated as a result of irritation at assertions that money was a "measure" of value. He noted that this notion presupposes and originates from a classical or objective value theory in which exchange involves the "reciprocal surrender of equivalent goods" (i.e., goods of equivalent value).[20] Neoclassical theory, he argued, interprets value subjectively, as the significance of marginal units of commodities to individuals when compared under a condition of scarcity, which comparisons imply *no* measurement, only *ranking*. Exchange is motivated precisely by *inequalities* in the subjective valuations (rankings) by individuals, of goods held by themselves and others.

> But subjective valuation, which is the pivot of all economic activity, only arranges commodities in order of their significance; it does not measure this significance....In a market, exchanges will continue until it is no longer possible for reciprocal surrender of commodities by any two individuals to result in their each

acquiring commodities that stand higher on their value scales than those surrendered....[21]

The equilibrium condition given in the last sentence quoted is certainly not as sophisticated a statement as that derived from indifference curve analysis, in which, with infinitely divisible goods, Parato optimality occurs where the ratios of the marginal utilities of the goods (and of marginal utility to price for each of the goods) are equal for the trading parties. Not only was this statement written in 1912, however; but given that real trade more often than not involves discrete goods, Mises' statement is more general and correct.

Indifference analysis also leads to the same conclusion Mises reached regarding money prices as a measure of satisfaction. For the individual in equilibrium the ratio of marginal utilities equals the price ratio (on the highest indifference curve attainable) for any pair of goods. The prices may be specified (after all, real prices can be observed), but the marginal utilities cannot. Only the *ratio* is the same, and since there is an *infinite* set of pairs of numbers representing marginal utilities yielding the same ratio, clearly *neither* of the prices in any sense *measures* the marginal utility of the goods associated.

Mises' contributions to the ordinal theory of value did not go *entirely* unrecognized, or at least uncriticized. Ellis responded to Mises in 1934. In his view goods had value in their own right, and the value of money was derived and existed in definite magnitudes. Thus he thought there was no objection to using it as a measure of absolute commodity values.[22] 1934, however, was the very year in which Hicks and Allen revived indifference analysis and used it to demonstrate the ordinality and nonmeasurability of utility.[23] Only five years later (1939) Hicks' *Value and Capital* completed and cemented the ordinal revolution.[24]

Also in 1934 another American economist, Alan R. Sweezy, published a study of Austrian value theory. Sweezy, however, was entirely concerned with criticizing from a positivist viewpoint the formal, tautological nature of subjective value theory in general, and in particular at the hands of Mises and some other Austrians. The measurability issue is mentioned briefly in one footnote, and then only to deny that such measurability, if discovered, would obviate the uselessness of utility theory.[25]

Ellis and Sweezy can be forgiven for failing to anticipate the advance of utility theory at the hands of Hicks and Allen (somewhat in the fashion of John Stuart Mill writing just before the marginal revolution that there was nothing left to add to value theory). In the light of that advance, however, they clearly should have given more consideration to Mises' arguments. At least Ellis and Sweezy were aware of those arguments. Hicks, to whom credit belongs for making the ordinal interpretation stick, lists only Pareto and Slutsky as progenitors, and specifically lists the Austrians with Jevons and Walras as giving utility a cardinal interpretation.[26] There may have been some subtle cross-fertilization here, however, as Hicks mentions Hayek, Mises' student, as among those who influenced his thinking on the matter. Hicks can be forgiven a lack of direct knowledge of *The Theory of Money and Credit* due to its late English publication.

Stigler, writing in 1950 on the history of utility theory, has less excuse than Hicks for a lack of awareness of Mises' contributions.[27] Like Hicks, Stigler also lists Pareto in 1906 as the first to give utility an ordinal interpretation,[28] though, as he also correctly notes, Pareto was inconsistent on the matter.[29] Stigler then lists W.E. Johnson in 1913,[30] and E.E. Slutsky in 1915[31] as helping secure the position that notions of measurable utility could be eliminated from economics. He goes on to say that *none* of the other leading economists of the day rejected the measurability of utility.[32] Clearly that is untrue.

To this day the major historians of economic thought appear unaware of Mises' contributions here. Mark Blaug, for example, makes no mention of it. Blaug does mention Sweezy's essay, but only as indicating the Austrian economists of the 1920s were developing an ordinal interpretation of utility,[33] an interpretation of Sweezy for which I find no evidence. Even more disconcerting is Schumpeter's neglect of Mises' contribution while citing Pareto, Johnson and Slutsky, as Schumpeter knew Mises well.[34] Mises' 1912 discussion is unambiguous to the point of militancy on the ordinal nature of utility and clearly deserves inclusion in the above list.

Having made his clarification of value theory, Mises felt it necessary, before dealing with the demand for money, to clearly define and clarify the components of the money stock. This was a subject on which there was some confusion for at least two reasons: (1) the change in monetary institutions and forms of money as banking practices changed, and (2) the use of the equation of exchange, verbally or mathematically, in monetary analysis.

Habits of thought engrained in periods when most money was metallic carried over into the period in which notes and deposits were emerging as claims on metallic reserves, in amounts *greater* than those reserves. This mental inertia resulted in retention of the term "money" as applying only to the metallic base. The status of notes and deposits was thus left ambiguous, even among monetary theorists, though such claims clearly affected economic activity in the same way as "money."[35] This combination of restricted definition and ambiguity clouded the connections between money and other economic variables, casting doubt on the validity of the quantity theory, as was often pointed out by its opponents.

The modern definition of money is more inclusive than the older definition. Money consists of currency and coin (whether full bodied or token) plus deposits. There are still some distinctions, between types of deposits for example, and ambiguities exist, but the concept is clearer for the elimination of meaningless distinctions. Mises was one of the earliest to develop the essentially modern concept. In the process he eliminated certain distinctions and made others which were necessary for further analysis.

He began by *apparently* retaining and even strengthening the original distinction by supplying the term "money substitutes" to refer to perfectly secure and immediately convertible claims (notes and deposits) to "money," remarking on the special suitability of such claims for use in exchange. He argued that three factors affected the value of a claim: (1) the value of the objects claimed, (2) the probability that the objects will actually be reclaimed, and (3) the time period, if any, after which redemption can take place. The *value* of *perfectly* secure and *immediately* convertible claims was, he argued, derivative of and equivalent to that of the objects claimed.[36]

While distinguishing between money and money substitutes, Mises denied as meaningless a distinction made by many economists between banknotes and token money on the one hand and deposits on the other, classifying the former but not the latter as money. In his view these were all money substitutes, without valid economic distinctions. He then made clear that his distinction between money and money substitutes, was itself purely analytical in purpose, listing several arguments for including *all* money substitutes in the money supply, and indicating his agreement with those arguments.[37]

The prime reason Mises wished to retain the distinction between money and money substitutes was in order to distinguish with regard to the latter category, in a situation of fractional reserves, between that portion "covered" by reserves and that which was not. Covered money substitutes he termed *money certificates*, and uncovered money substitutes he termed *fiduciary media*.[38] This distinction becomes important for further analysis of many topics in monetary and business cycle theory, as will be seen in later chapters.

With regard to money proper, Mises distinguished three categories: commodity money, a term he preferred over "metallic" money since the latter would include token money he saw as a money substitute, involved the use of a commodity in the technological sense as money; *credit money* consisted of circulating media which were claims on physical or legal persons, where such claims were *not* both payable on demand and perfectly secure; *fiat money* was money with a special legal qualification (in essence nonconvertible legal tender currency), the material composition of which was not a significant factor in its use as money.[39]

With these definitions, and recognizing that money certificates simply replace "money" in people's cash balances, Mises distinguished between the stock of money in a broad and in a narrow sense. The former consisted of the sum of money and money substitutes held by individuals, and the latter referred only to money proper held. In a community using money substitutes where the banking system operates on fractional reserves, he pointed out, either the reserves or money certificates must be excluded to avoid double counting. Excluding reserves, the money supply in the broad sense would consist, in Mises' terms, of the sum of money proper minus reserves and plus money substitutes held.[40] Where in modern times money consists of fiat currency, token coins and credit money with fractional reserves, Mises' definitions and procedure yield a money supply essentially equivalent to the current definitions.[41]

Mises has received very little credit for his conceptual clarification of the components and nature of the money stock. Ellis does mention Mises' contribution here, and says that his method is "clearly superior" to the older practice.[42] He further mentions that Hawtry,[43] Keynes[44] and Robertson[45] subsequently adopted the practice of defining money inclusively. As Ephrime Eshag points out, however, this was no doubt due to Marshall's influence (they were his students), even though Marshall himself never quite made that transition in thought.[46]

Stock Demand Analysis

Perhaps more important than pointing out that Mises' definition of the money supply equates to the modern definition, is to show that he saw both the demand for and supply of money in *stock* terms, as witness the following statements.

> Every economic agent is obliged to hold a stock of the common medium of exchange sufficient to cover his probable business and personal requirements....[47]

> The individual's demand and stock of money are the basis of the demand and stock in the whole community. So long as there are no money substitutes in use, the social demand for money and the social stock of money are merely the respective sums of the individual demands and stocks....[48]

and even more clearly,

> The stock of money of the community is the sum of the stocks of the individuls; there is no such thing as errant money, no money which even for a moment does not form part of somebody's stock....[49]

38

The shift from viewing the demand for and supply of money in *flow* terms to viewing them in stock terms is one of the crucial advances in monetary theory in this century. For one thing it eliminates the confusion between demand and supply involved in viewing the left side of the equation of exchange (MV or money times velocity, where velocity is the average rate of turnover per unit of money) as the "supply" of money (strictly, the "amount supplied" in some time period).

Further, viewing demand as the demand to hold a stock of money focuses attention on the crucial issues of how people *evaluate* units of money in deciding the size of their stock, and therefore aids in solving the problem of the determination of the value of money. One aspect of this is modern portfolio balance analysis, which considers how individuals compare, at the margin, money stocks with other stocks of liquid wealth.[50]

Some of the advantages of the stock approach were beginning to be grasped by a few economists around the turn of the century. Wicksell's *Interest and Prices* (1898) was based on an explicit cash balance approach, and indeed recognized and analyzed the demand for money to hold in terms of *real* balances.[51] With regard to the money supply, Wicksell correctly saw the total stock as equivalent to the cash balances of individuals, though he maintained (along with many other economists) an untenable distinction between "hoards" and "circulating balances."[52] Wicksell also distinguished between money seen as coin and notes on the other hand and credit (deposit money) on the other. That he did not quite escape the confusions of the flow concept is indicated by the fact that he saw an extension of credit as increasing the *velocity* rather than the quantity of money, on the theory that credit simply transferred money.[53]

Irving Fisher, in *The Purchasing Power of Money* (1911), also distinguished deposit money, designated M' in his equation, from money proper, designated M. He attributed to M' its own velocity V'. The equation of exchange then became $MV + M'V' = PT$ (where T = the sum of the transactions occurring during the implied time period), which at least avoids Wicksell's confusion over an increase in credit.[54] In general, Fisher's sole reliance on the flow approach embodied in the equation of exchange, despite mathematical and analytic innovations, was a retrogression from

Wickell's cash balance method. Karl Helfferich's monetary treatise, which appeared just after the turn of the century, followed Wicksell's approach, but also repeated his errors discussed above.[55]

In assessing the validity of the quantity theory interpreted as a proportional direct response of prices to a change in the quantity of money proper, maintaining the distinction between M and M' led both Fisher and Wicksell, along with Cassel and a host of lesser authors, into a morass of futile theorizing on the stability of the relations between the two and reliance on a ceteris paribus assumption.[56] One advantage of the method of Mises and current theorists, of simply defining money inclusively, is to eliminate this issue.

After *The Theory of Money and Credit*, an explicit cash-balance approach based on a transformation of the equation of exchange from $MV = PQ$ (where $Q =$ The Quantity of Goods and services) to $M = 1/V \, PQ$, or in real balance terms, $M/P = KQ$ (where $1/V = K$), began to appear in publications of Cambridge economists. Marshall had developed a stock concept of the demand for money in unpublished essays written in the last quarter of the 19th Century, and he passed this method of analysis on to his students.[57] Anglo-Saxon economists, with a few exceptions such as Ellis and Patinkin, have tended to attribute the acceptance of the notion of the demand for and supply of money in stock terms to and date it from those Cambridge publications, either Marshall in 1923,[58] Edwin Cannan in 1921,[59] or A. C. Pigou in 1917.[60]

There appears to be more than a touch of Anglo-Saxon bias in this construction of doctrinal history. In the hands of Wicksell, Helfferich and Mises there appears to have been established a Germanic tradition of cash balance analysis, in print long before Cambridge authors. Indeed Mises attributes this approach to Menger.[61] None of these Germanic authors other than Mises, however, attempted to fully integrate monetary and value theory. In doing so Mises gave cash balance analysis a surprisingly modern form, which he then rigorously applied to the problems and issues of monetary theory.

One last preliminary argument of Mises', which concerns the nature of money, may be mentioned here because it indicates a possible weakness with the analysis he was to make on the demand for money. In a chapter on money as an economic good, Mises rhetorically asked whether money was a consumption or a production good. His opinion was that it fell into neither of those categories. Indeed, he rejected the notion that it was a consumption good without further argument, as if that was obvious. Whether money was a production good or not was apparently less obvious. Many people had asserted that it should be considered a production good, equivalent to "transport" since it transfers goods.[62]

Mises' denial of this reasoning was trenchant: "transfer" and "transport" often occur together, but they are distinct and not equivalent categories. If either production or consumption goods change in quantity the wealth of society changes, but that cannot be said about money; changes in its quantity result in changes in its value leaving human welfare unchanged.[63] In other words, changes in the *nominal* quantity of money result in changes in prices which tend to restore the original *real* quantity, leaving people no better or worse off. It followed, Mises thought, that any quantity of money would suffice for society's needs.[64]

One objection to this argument can be dealt with rather rapidly. The argument seems to contradict the modern argument attributable to Friedman that there is an optimum quantity of money.[65] The "optimum quantity" of money referred to, however, is the quantity of *real* balances held by individuals, which *is* a component of wealth. The argument recognizes that the costs of holding real balances are affected by the price behavior conditioned by the rate of growth of the nominal money supply, and seeks to specify that rate of growth (of nominal money) which will result in optimum real balances being held.

In the simplest version of the argument, where the private cost of holding cash is the interest forgone, and the social cost of producing (nominal) money is zero, the optimum real balances will be held at that rate of deflation which makes the nominal rate of interest zero. This is because, with the cost per dollar of

41

(fiat) money production being (virtually) zero, the optimum quantity of real balances is the maximum, which occurs where the marginal utility of holding money (which must equal the opportunity cost in equilibrium) is zero.

In some respects Mises' and Friedman's arguments here are similar. To Mises, increasing the quantity of money simply results in neutralizing price changes, and hence no additional benefits. In Friedman's analysis, excess monetary growth reduces real balances, so some of the benefits of such balances are *lost*. Also, *no* optimum quantity of *nominal* money is implied in Friedman's argument, but only an optimum *growth rate*. Since any quantity of money can grow at any rate, Mises was quite correct in saying that any quantity of money would do. What is more, if Mises' argument is interpreted as advocating a stable nominal money supply, it reaches the same result as Friedman's. This is because, in an economy in which the real interest rate and the annual real growth rate are historically very similar, producing a rate of deflation sufficient to reduce the nominal interest rate to zero would require a growth rate in the nominal money supply that was virtually zero.

The impression Mises' argument gives, however, that money is so completely neutral that none of its quantitative variations affect real variables, is not only incorrect (as Friedman's argument shows), but is out of character with much of what he wrote elsewhere. It is justifiable only as a statement of long run comparative statics, and was clearly intended as such. He went on to thoroughly analyze the distributional effects of monetary fluctuations in the adjustment period.

Mises' apparent failure here, in not seeing the issue in terms of real balances whose quantitive alterations *do* change wealth, and in not seeing through the "quantity" of money to the growth rate, are certainly forgivable to an economist writing just after the turn of the century. (Indeed, nobody seems to have thought about optimum *real* balances before Friedman.) It raises a question, however, which is fundamental in the next chapter: How clearly did Mises distinguish between the utility of money and the utility of the *services* of money? His too quick rejection of the notion of money as a *consumption* good indicates the same possible weakness. Money obviously *is* a consumption good which yields its services when being *held*, not just when spent. Consumption does not *mean* destruction. Houses also yield services while being held (occupied), even if they are later sold. This would be no less true if a doubling of the quantity of houses caused their prices to drop fifty percent.

The problem here is probably a simple lapse in awareness of things Mises showed clear understanding of elsewhere. It will later be shown that Mises *was* aware that the price behavior associated with various monetary growth rates altered desired real balances by altering the costs of holding money. He was in fact one of the originators of this analysis, which followed quite logically from his particular method of applying marginal utility theory to the demand for money.

Notes

[1]Knut Wicksell, Joseph Schumpeter, Karl Helfferich, and L. Albert Hann among others all denied the applicability of marginal utility theory to the demand for money on the basis of the assumed circularity discussed in Chapter 3 below. See Howard Ellis, *German Monetary Theory*, 1905-1933 (Cambridge Ma.: Harvard University Press, 1934): 51-52, 63. For Helfferich's Discussion, see his *Money* (London: Ernest Benn Ltd., 1927): 526-527, originally published as *Das Geld* (Leipzig: C.L. Herschfeld, 1903).

[2]This is one of the clearest examples of the use of a straw man in monetary literature. Both Mises and Ellis remark that it is difficult to find an economist who fits this definition. See Ludwig von Mises, *The Theory of Money and Credit* (Indianapolis: Liberty Classics, 1981): 515, and *German Monetary Theory*: 91.

[3]Robert Liefmann, *Geld und Gold* (Stuttgart: Deutsche verlags-anstalt, 1916): Chapter 4.

[4]Ernst Wageman, *Allgemeine Geldlehre* (Berlin: H.R. Englemann, 1923): 86-88.

[5]See Don Roper, "Late Nineteenth Century U.S. Monetary History and the Monetary Theory of an Open Economy" (unpublished manuscript, University of Utah, June 1977).

[6]Georg Friedrich Knapp, *Staatliche Theorie des Geldes* (Leipzig: Dunker and Humblot, 1905).

[7]For a less charitible interpretation See F.A. Hayek, *Denationalization of Money* (London: Institute of Economic Affairs, 1976): 26.

[8]*Principles of Economics*: 357-371.

[9]F.A. Hayek, *The Counter-Revolution of Science* (Glenco, Illinois: The Free Press, 1952): 82-83.

[10]*The Theory of Money and Credit*: 43-44.

[11]Ibid., 126. This is sufficient to disprove the charge that Mises was a metallist.

[12]Ibid., 45-46.

[13]Ibid., 46-48.

[14]Ibid., 84-86. The function of a gold clause was to protect both creditor and debtor against changes in the value of money over the period of a credit transaction through a crude form of indexing. Since the amount being borrowed, given the price of gold at the time a loan was made or bond sold, could be specified as an amount of gold, the amount to be repaid could be specified as the value, at the time of repayment, of an amount of gold larger than the initial amount by interest over the period of the

44

loan. Gold clauses in credit contracts were common before the great depression, and though outlawed in 1935, are now legal again. Their infrequent current use is probably a result of both unfamiliarity with such clauses on the part of the public, and greater current awareness that the real value of gold is itself subject to large fluctuations.

[15] Ibid., 83.

[16] Ibid., 87-89.

[17] *German Monetary Theory*: 77-78.

[18] Arthur Nussbaum, *Das Geld in Theorie und Praxis des Deutschen und ausländischen Rechts* (Tübingen: Mohr, 1925: 18-19.

[19] *Notes and Recollections*: 56.

[20] *The Theory of Money and Credit*: 51.

[21] Ibid., 52-53, and Ludwig von Mises, *Theorie des Geldes und der Umlaufsmittel* (Munich and Leipzig: Duncker and Humblot, 1912): 16, hereafter cited as *Theorie des Geldes*.

[22] *German Monetary Theory*: 80.

[23] See J. R. Hicks, "A Reconsideration of the Theory of Value, Part I," *Economica*, n.s., 1 (February 1934): 52-76, and R.D.G. Allen, "A Reconsideration of the Theory of Value, Part II," *Economica*, n.s., 1 (May 1934): 196-219. Actually, Allen began the revival of indifference analysis the year previous to this, in his "The Nature of Indifference Curves," *Review of Economic Studies* 1 (February 1933): 110-121.

[24] Citations in this work will be to J. R. Hicks, *Value and Capital*, 2d ed. (Oxford: Clarenden Press, 1946).

[25] Alan R. Sweezy, "The Interpretation of Subjective Value in the Writings of the Austrian Economists," *Review of Economic Studies* 1 (June 1934): 176-185.

[26] *Value and Capital*: 17-19.

[27] George Stigler, "The Development of Utility Theory II," *Journal of Political Economy* 18 (August 1950): 373-396.

[28] Vilfredo Parato, *Manuel d'economie politique* (Milan: Societa editrice Libraries, 1906).

[29] To quote Stigler, "The Manual is strewn with passages that are meaningful only if utility is measurable...." Stigler, "The Development of Utility Theory II": 383.

[30] W. E. Johnson, "The Pure Theory of Utility Curves," *Economic Journal* 23 (December 1913): 483-513.

[31] E.E. Slutsky, "Sulla teoria del bilancio des consumatore," *Gionale degle economisti* 51 (1915): 1-26.

[32] Stigler, "The Development of Utility Theory II": 383.

[33] Mark Blaug, *Economic Theory in Retrospect*, 3rd ed. (Cambridge: Cambridge University Press, 1978): 388.

[34] Joseph Schumpeter, *History of Economic Analysis* (New York: Oxford University Press, 1954): 1063-1065. Of course Mises' students, particularly Murray Rothbard, have recognized his early development of ordinal utility theory. See Murray N. Rothbard, "The Austrian Theory of Money," in Edwin G. Dolan, ed., *The Foundations of Modern Austrian Economics* (Kansas City: Sheed and Ward, 1976): 160-161. Orthodox Doctrinal Historians have thus far paid no attention, however.

[35] *The Theory of Money and Credit*: 65.

[36] Ibid., 63-66.

[37]Ibid., 66.

[38]Ibid., 155.

[39]Ibid., 71-76.

[40]Mises actually stated this the other way around, excluding certificates and defining the stock of and demand for money in the broad sense to include money proper including cover (reserves) plus fiduciary media. See Ibid., 155-156, and *Theorie des Geldes*: 144-145.

[41]Since he was thinking of checking deposits the modern equivalent would be M_1.

[42]*German Monetary Theory*: 162.

[43]R.G. Hawtrey, *Currency and Credit* (London: Longmans, Green and Co., 1919): 1-52.

[44]John Maynard Keynes, *A Treatise on Money* (New York: Harcourt, Brace 1930): the first two chapters. Oddly enough, proof exists that Keynes had read *The Theory of Money and Credit* before this, as he had reviewed it (somewhat favorably, in fact) in the *Economic Journal*. See Keynes, "Review of *Theorie des Geldes und der Umlaufsmittel* by Ludwig von Mises and of *Geld und Kapital* by Friedrich Bendixen," *Economic Journal* 24 (September 1914): 417.

[45]D. H. Robertson, *Money* (New York: Harcourt, Brace, 1922): chapter 3.

[46]Ephrime Eshag, *From Marshall to Keynes: An Essay on the Monetary Theory of the Cambridge School* (New York: Augustus M. Kelley, 1965): 8-10, 22. What Marshall had done was to claify the numerical relationship which exists between bank reserves and deposits, expanding on Sir Robert Giffen's earlier analysis. This made it natural for Marshall's students to develop an inclusive definition of money, as Eshag argues. However, influence by Mises cannot be ruled out (see note 44 above).

[47]*The Theory of Money and Credit*: 154, and *Theorie des Geldes*: 142.

[48]*The Theory of Money and Credit*: 155, and *Theorie des Geldes*: 143.

[49]*The Theory of Money and Credit*: 170, and *Theorie des Geldes*: 161.

[50]Mises did not get very far with the portfolio balance aspect (see chapter 3, note 31, and also chapter 6 for his objections to treating interest as the cost of holding money). The seminal essay on portfolio balance came later in the form of J.R. Hicks, "A suggestion for Simplifying the Theory of Money," *Economica*, n.s. 2 (February 1935): 1-19.

[51]Knut Wicksell, *Interest and Prices* (English translation of *Geldzins und güterpreise*, trans. by R.F. Kahn, New York: Augustus M. Kelley, 1962, originally Jena: Gustav Fischer, 1898): 38-50.

[52]The distinction is untenable for several reasons. For one, all balances "circulate" in the sense that they have a turnover period in which every unit is replaced. The only difference is one of degree, in longer or shorter turnover periods, that is, larger or smaller balances *ceteris paribus*. For another thing, in *no* other sense do *any* balances circulate. As Mises pointed out, there is no period of time in which a unit of money is not in someone's cash balance. Also, the term "hoard" is somewhat odious from the viewpoint of positive economics since it implies a value judgement as to the appropriate size of money balances.

[53]*Interest and Prices*: 42. It is indicative that even in his later work, in which Wicksell realized that the "average period of idleness," K (the proportion of real or nominal

income in some time period that is held in the form of a real or nominal cash balance), is the reciprocal of V (velocity, the average rate of turnover), all of his analysis of the determinants of K ran in terms of the determinants of V. That his analysis contained insights is undeniable. He discussed such factors as transactions, vertical integration and payment habits. As in *Interest and Prices*, he argued once again that credit amounts to a transfer of money, increasing V (not M). However, not only is it better to see notes and deposits as components of M, but in all of this the size of people's cash balances simply falls out from the determinants of the rate of *spending*. It never quite occurred to Wicksell to think directly in terms of the determinants of desired money balances. Only then does the theory of the demand for money become choice-theoretic in the same sense as that of the demands for other commodities. See Wicksell, *Lectures on Political Economy* vol. 2 (New York: Macmillan, 1935): Chapter 3.

[54]Irving Fisher, *The Purchasing Power of Money* (New York: Macmillan, 1911): 33-54.

[55]Helfferich, *Money*: 151, 455-461.

[56]None of these authors were happy with this situation. Cassel remarks that an increase in money may itself influence both velocity and the relation between cash and bank money. See Gustav Cassel, *The Theory of Social Economy* (New York: Harcourt, Brace, 1924): 459. And Fisher writes that the inclusion of deposit circulation in the equation of exchange means the influence exerted by money on prices is less direct, and that some economists argue that it breaks the connection altogether. See Fisher, *The Purchasing Power of Money*: 49-50.

[57]In fact the stock concept first appears in Marshall's work in a manuscript dated 1871, and appears throughout subsequent work. See Eshag, *From Marshall to Keynes*: 3-8. As Eshag also notes here, however, Marshall often carried out monetary analysis in terms of the classical version of the quantity theory.

[58]Alfred Marshall *Money, Credit and Commerce* (London: Macmillan, 1923).

[59]Edwin Cannan, "The Application of the Theoretical Apparatus of Supply and Demand to units of Currency," *Economic Journal* 31 (December 1921): 453-461.

[60]A.C. Pigou, "The Value of Money," *Quarterly Journal of Economics* 32 (November 1917): 38-65.

[61]Notes and Recollections: 57.

[62]This viewpoint has not disappeared. Friedman argues that real cash balances are at least in part of a factor of production. See Milton Friedman, "The Optimum Quantity of Money," in Friedman, *The Optimum Quantity of Money and Other Essays* (Chicago: Aldine Publishing Co., 1969): 14.

[63]*The Theory of Money and Credit*: 95-102.

[64]Despite denying in this fashion that money was a capital good in the sense of having physical productivity, Mises admitted that money was an element of *private* capital to the extent that it constituted a means by which an individual could obtain other capital goods. See Ibid., 107.

[65]"The Optimum Quantity of Money," in Friedman, *The Optimum Quantity of Money and Other Essays*: 1-50.

3
THE REGRESSION THEOREM AND
THE DEMAND FOR MONEY

Introduction

Though *The Theory of Money and Credit* is virtually encyclopedic in its coverage of the problems of monetary theory, Mises considered the integration of monetary and value theory by the application of marginal analysis to the demand for money to be the central problem, and his solution to be the most important contribution of his book. That solution involved classic Austrian analysis and has been subjected to more than a little criticism, as we shall see. In recent years Don Patinkin has developed an alternative solution to the problem Mises dealt with. Patinkin's analysis, however, is purely Walrasian in nature. The function of this chapter is to explicate the basic problem and Mises' solution, deal with some objections to Mises' arguments, then contrast Mises' and Patinkin's analyses. A final comment on the recurrence of the basic problem will also be included.

The Austrian Circle and
the Regression Theorem

It was mentioned in the last chapter that many prominent economists of Mises' day denied the possibility of applying marginal utility theory to the demand for money. The resulting dichotomy not only shunted much of monetary theory into unproductive lines, but called neoclassic value theory itself into question, since its greatest claim to superiority over classical value theory was its greater generality. Classical theory had no difficulty explaining the value of both goods and money on the same basis, at least as long as fiat and token money could be ignored (though of course they cannot be), since the value of *commodity money* could be explained by reference to its cost of production just as the value of other commodities were.

The basic problem motivating the denials was known as the "Austrian circle" and involved the appearance that any attempt to apply marginal utility reasoning to the demand for money was circular. As Helfferich explained it, money can only have utility to individuals if it has real value, that is, purchasing power, but that can only be known if the price level is determined. Thus in even speaking of the marginal utility of money one assumes what is to be explained.[1]

Mises explained the difficulty in greater detail. Subjective estimates of individuals, he argued, are the basis of the value of money just as with other goods. There is an important difference between the two, however, The utility or "subjective use value" of goods depends both on external facts (the causal connection between goods and human wants stressed by Menger[2]), which Mises termed their "objective use values," and on their position on human value scales.[3] That is to say, since goods have causal ability to satisfy human desires, and are scarce, individuals rank units on their value scales. By such analysis the phenomena of value and price are explained without *prior* reference to price ("objective exchange value").[4]

In the case of money, however, all of its uses (and hence any utility from such uses) depend on its being used as a medium of exchange, and hence having purchasing power. For money, the "subjective use value and subjective exchange value (the utility of whatever it can be traded for) coincide," and "both are derived from its objective exchange value."[5]

Buttressing this point Mises makes a statement which has been severely criticized. First he quotes Wieser (from *Natural Value*) as saying that "the exchange value of money is the anticipated use value of the things that can be obtained for it."[6] In another place Mises adds his endorsement to Wieser's statement:

The price of money, like other prices, is determined by the subjective valuations of buyers and sellers. But, as has been said already, the subjective use value of money, which coincides with its subjective exchange value, is nothing but the anticipated use-value of the things which are to be bought with it. The subjective value of money must be measured by the marginal utility of the goods for which the money can be exchanged.[7]

It is crucial to note that *immediately* following *both* statements he says that, therefore, people can only place valuations on money (and I shall argue that he means valuations for purposes of *holding* in cash balances) on the assumption that money has a certain purchasing power.

The bottom line of the argument is clear. One cannot explain the value of a unit of money by supply and demand (even if they are correctly interpreted in stock terms) while deriving the demand curve by an analytical process which necessarily presumes that money already has a value without being involved in circular reasoning. As Mises put it:

The marginal utility of money to any individual, that is, the marginal utility derivable from the goods that can be obtained with the given quantity of money or that must be surrendered for the required money, presupposes a certain exchange value of the money; so the latter cannot be derived from the former.[8]

This was the basic dilemma accepted by continental monetary theorists for several decades.

Mises' method of escaping the circularity, correct or incorrect, was certainly ingenious. It consisted of explicitly introducing time and causality into the matter in classic Austrian fashion. It is true, he agreed, that valuation of money presupposes an existing exchange value. But the value to be explained, which is today's exchange value and is determined by supply and demand today, is not the same as the value presupposed in the construction of the individual and market demand curves, which is yesterday's exchange value.[9] Mises termed this the regression theorem.

That people construct demand curves for money today based on past prices, and hence that past and present prices are linked, is a bold hypothesis, but as a theory of the determination of the value of money it appears at first merely to push the problem back. The value of money yesterday must also depend on a demand for money yesterday which was constructed using the exchange value money had the day *before* yesterday. Mises points out, however, that this regression is not infinite: it only goes back to the first time a money was used *as* money. On that day its value as money (demand) must have been based on its value as a commodity in *direct* use the day previously.[10]

With the regression theorem Mises thought he had solved several problems. First, he had escaped the Austrian circle. Second, he had provided a deductive proof of Menger's hypothesis concerning the emergence of money (discussed above in chapter 2). Third, he thought he had explained, by this inherently necessary continuity element in demand, not only the value of commodity money, but also that of credit and fiat monies.[11] Mises' theory of the demand for money has been subject to some criticism, which basically falls into two categories. The first category deals with his explanation of the basis on which units of money are valued, and the second deals directly with the regression theorem itself. These criticisms will be dealt with in that order.

Evaluation of Money and Demand: Objections

Both Patinkin and, more recently, Moss,[12] have criticized Mises for equating the marginal utility of money with the marginal utility of the goods it can purchase. The mistake here, as Patinkin puts it, is that our concern should be with the utility of *holding* money, not with that of *spending* it.[13] If correct this is a significant criticism, and Mises certainly did say in the statements quoted in the last section that the subjective value of money is the anticipated use value of the things it can buy, but what did he mean?

In context, and given the statements immediately following those quotations, a reasonable interpretation is simply that people cannot decide whether to add a unit of money to a cash balance or spend it unless one can compare its marginal utility as reserve purchasing power with that in exchange, which is *indeed* the subjective value of the goods it can purchase, and such comparison requires that the unit of currency have purchasing power.[14]

The entire context of Mises' discussion unequivocally bears on the derivation of the individual and market demands for money to *hold* as a *stock*. It is just as unequivocal that what is ultimately being demanded is *real* balances, as witness the following statements:

> And he whose demand for money is less than his stock of it will behave in an exactly contrary fashion. If an individual's stock of money diminishes (his property or income remaining the same), then he will take steps to reach the desired level of reserve purchasing power by suitable behavior in making sales and purchases.[15]

> Those who participate in exchange transactions, and consequently desire to acquire or dispose of money, do not value the monetary unit solely with regard to the fact that they can use it in other acts of exchange, but also because they require money in order to pay taxes, to transfer borrowed capital and pay interest, and to make presents. They consider the level of their purchasing power reserves with a view to the necessity of having money ready for all these purposes, and their judgement as to the extent of their requirements for money is what decides the demand for money with which they enter the market.[16]

Though Mises confused the issue by saying that "the subjective value of money is the marginal utility of the goods it can buy," and indeed may have had lapses in distinguishing between the utility of money and the utility of the services of money (see the last part of chapter 2), it appears clear that he ultimately had in mind the utility of *holding* money.[17]

At this point another criticism in the first category becomes relevant. Ellis charged Mises with attaching utility to nominal units of money, which Ellis accepts as circular, rather than to real units of value.[18] Moss makes the same basic charge, though his version is more subtle and precise due to accumulated monetary knowledge over the interim, when he says that Mises failed to put real balances themselves in the utility function as Patinkin did.[19]

If the interpretation of Mises' arguments I have given above is correct, however, Ellis and Moss are simply incorrect. If a unit of money has a value, then the individual can, for an additional unit of money income, compare the marginal utilities of the additional present or future goods obtainable with that of adding that unit's worth of purchasing power to his/her cash balance, and it is precisely the magnitude of *real* balances that Mises is talking about determining by such a marginal calculation. The individual simply expresses that demand by demanding nominal units of money with a given purchasing power each.

In evidence of their criticism Ellis and Moss point to certain arguments of Mises' which require some background. Mises was an advocate of the quantity theory as long as it was interpreted properly as a theory of the determination of the value of money by stock supply and demand "correctly" derived. He was very critical of mechanical versions of the theory, and particularly of all assertions of proportionality. Mises repeatedly stressed that money does not enter circulation by equiproportional additions to everyone's cash balances, but enters certain people's balances first and spreads out from there, inevitably altering relative prices and redistributing wealth, and causing nonproportional increases in prices.[20]

Mises went on, however, to deny that proportionality in price increases would result even if the money supply *was* expanded by an equiproportional addition to everyone's cash balance (everyone getting a dollar for each one already possessed, or for each ten, etc.). Such proportionality, he argued, would require that variations in the marginal utility of money were inversely proportional to those in the quantity of money, but there was no reason to suppose individual valuations worked this way, and every reason to suppose they did not.[21]

Ellis asserts that Mises confused money and real value here. Doubling the latter doesn't necessarily produce an inversely proportional decline in marginal utility, but doubling the former makes real balances (to use Patinkin's term) twice as large as desired at existing prices, and the desired real balances will only be restored when expenditure has made prices double.[22] Note that from Ellis' 1930s perspective the stock demand for nominal balances is rectangularly hyperbolic.

Moss believes he sees the same basic error. In his view a rectangularly hyperbolic stock demand for nominal balances (which Mises is here *denying*) is implicit in Mises' own arguments.

54

If an individual demands a certain real balance, and simply adjusts nominal balances to maintain that level of purchasing power, then doubling nominal balances *would* halve the utility of the monetary unit. Moss then notes that the only way to escape this is to make real balances themselves subject to utility calculations.[23]

It is clear that both Moss and Ellis interpret Mises' theory as saying that the individual values units of money only with a view to maintaining a predecided and given level of desired purchasing power, and that utility calculation is not applied to the level of real balances. From this perspective they find his nonproportionality argument contradictory. It does not occur to them that his nonproportionality argument is evidence *against* their interpretation of his theory of the demand for money. Consider:

> Here, as in all departments of economic life, it is the subjective valuations of the separate economic agents that alone are decisive. The store of purchasing power held by two such agents whose objective economic circumstances were identical might be quite different if the advantages and disadvantages of such a store were estimated differently by the different agents.[24]

It was precisely by considering the subjective determinants of *real* balances that Patinkin was able to demonstrate that the demand for nominal balances was *less* than unitarily elastic. This was because *either* a change in P with M constant (initially), or a change in M with P constant (initially), changes real wealth and hence changes the quantity of real balances demanded in the same direction (on the assumption that real balances are a normal good). Therefore, only doubling *both* M *and* P would halve the marginal utility of the monetary unit, and only the "market equilibrium curve" defined by such proportional changes in M and P (leaving M/P unchanged) is a rectangular hyperbola.[25]

In the passages Moss and Ellis criticize, Mises was specifically considering an (equiproportional) increase in M with P initially constant, and asking whether the resulting expenditure would cause P to rise proportionately. If his assertion that the marginal utility of money did not vary in inverse proportion to its quantity referred to the initial situation (before expenditure drives prices up), it is correct: a doubling of *real* balances would *not* halve the marginal utility of the monetary unit. Where Mises erred was in assuming that it followed that prices would not rise proportionately with M. This would occur because, as prices increased, real balances would decline, reversing all of the initial wealth effects, until equilibrium was attained at the initial level of real balances *ceteris paribus*.

Oddly, in the argument discussed at the end of chapter 2, Mises had specifically asserted that a change in M would result in a proportional change in P, and that this would leave human welfare unchanged.[26] His nonproportionality argument contradicts this. However, a failure to step from a non-rectangularly-hyperbolic demand for nominal balances to the rectangularly-hyperbolic market equilibrium curve does *not* constitute evidence that Mises was "attaching marginal utility to nominal units of money" and not considering the demand for real balances.

Subjective Determinants of
Real Balances Demanded

It is easy to show that Mises explicitly discussed most of the subjective determinants of the stock demand for real balances listed by modern monetary theorists, and discussed them in that context. One of the fundamental motives he listed was the transactions demand, which, he argued, increased with the growth and extent of the division of labor.[27] Perhaps the most important reason Mises found for holding money, however, was uncertainty concerning future transactions and other contingencies.[28] In later work Mises decided that uncertainty as an ontological phenomenon was the prime reason for the holding of all economic stocks, including money balances.[29]

It was because of Mises' emphasis on the volume of transactions and on uncertainty as motives for holding money that Moss concluded Mises saw the demand for real balances as constant and given by the structure of the world, though Moss admitted that "Mises nowhere stated this exactly."[30] He went on to say that Mises did not consider real balances a function of either wealth or the interest rate, though in footnotes he again listed contrary statements.[31] In response I believe one should consider the quotation assigned footnote 15 above, in which Mises

56

explicitly lists both wealth (property) and income as determinates of *real* balances. He does not state the signs of the partials, but Mises was never one to state the obvious.

As for the interest rate, Mises' attitude was different from that developed by current monetary theory. He did not generally regard interest foregone as the cost of holding money. Though at one point, as Moss noted, he does seem to imply an inverse relation between the interest rate and the demand for money,[32] he generally argued that there was no direct connection between the two. There was only an indirect connection due to alterations in the distribution of wealth associated with fluctuations in the money supply (forced saving, etc.). His basic attitude was the classic one of long-run interest rate neutrality, based on a view that the rate of interest and the demand for money had essentially different determinants.[33]

Last, Moss himself is aware of Mises' clear and extensive discussion of the effects of inflationary expectations on the demand for money.[34] Thus, even if uncertainty is taken as underlying and given, and income is used as a surrogate for transactions, the list of determinants of the demand for real balances discussed or at least mentioned by Mises includes income, wealth, the interest rate (in the short run), and inflationary expectations. This list is too extensive, and Mises is too clear on the matter to sustain any assertion that he did not apply subjective cost and benefit considerations to the demand for real balances.[35]

Criticism and Defense of the Regression Theorem

Mises' regression theorem has been even more universally criticized than the other elements of his explanation of the utility of money just discussed. Indeed, almost no other economist has quite been willing to accept it, though the American William A. Scott either adopted it or discovered it independently some years later.[36] Among current economists only Murray Rothbard seems to be a whole-hearted advocate of the regression theorem.[37]

The first major critic of the theorem was Benjamin M. Anderson, who became a good friend of Mises. Anderson had considered and rejected a similar approach applied to general value theory in one of his earlier works. While impressed with Mises' logic and knowledge, he rejected the theorem as a mere historical account and argued that a logical explanation of present forces was needed to explain an existing situation.[38] Ellis approved this criticism but added little to it.[39]

This criticism seems to have missed the mark. Mises was indeed explaining the present value of money by present supply and demand, and merely deriving present demand by reference to people's present value rankings based on the prior purchasing power of money. Later in the same work Anderson himself admitted the essence of the theorem, that value from some other source than monetary employment is an essential precondition of the emergence of something as money,[40] as Mises pointed out in the 1924 edition of the *Theorie des Geldes und der Umlaufsmittel*.

Mises gave an expanded response to Anderson and Ellis in *Human Action*. He argued that while the phenomena described by the regression theorem were actual historical phenomena, it was not a historical explanation, attempting to explain a particular event by reference to specific historical antecedents. It was in fact a theoretical explanation of all the phenomena in the same class by reference to a general set of rules.[41]

J.C. Gilbert, echoing a criticism by Ellis of Mises' assertion that fiat money always emerged by suspension of convertibility, complained that the regression theorem did not explain how a new paper money could be introduced when the previous monetary system breaks down.[42] The easy response, however, is that *only* the regression theorem explains this. Such new currencies are always introduced at some fixed rate of exchange to the previous depreciated currency, so that the continuity element necessary for continuing demand is maintained.[43]

The Walrasian Solution to the Circularity Problem

The Cambridge authors who developed and disseminated cash balance analysis after Mises never seem to have been aware of the circularity problem. When Patinkin began writing *Money, Interest and Prices* he felt impelled to deal with the issue, though he saw it as a false problem. Summarizing Helfferich's version of the problem, Patinkin admitted that the marginal utility of money, unlike other goods, could not be determined unless prices were first specified, but argued that this is irrelevant to specification of demand functions.[44]

To see what the argument is about, consider an indifference map of a Hicksian variety in which all goods but money are considered as a single composite commodity (on the assumption that their relative prices do not vary, so their money prices all vary proportionately) and placed on one axis, while money is placed on the other. With the indifference curves given, we are prepared to conduct what Patinkin termed an "individual experiment." We give the individual a specific quantity of the goods (in Walrasian terms, an "initial endowment"), then by *varying* the price (value) of money in terms of the composite commodity and noting the subsequent optimizing tangencies a demand (and "excess" demand) curve for money can be derived for the individual and, by aggregation, for the market.

At this point we can conduct what Patkin termed a "market experiment," in which the demand curve and the money stock determine the value of money, *and hence the specific quantities demanded by individuals* (and hence the marginal utility of money). "Clearly," Patinkin says, "there is no circularity in stating that the market excess-demand equations derived from such experiments are then used to determine the equilibrium money prices of the market experiment."[45] He concludes that the whole circularity problem is a sham resulting from the elementary failure to distinguish between "demand" and "quantity demanded."

Patinkin's demonstration, the essence of which consists in showing that a *specific* value of money need not be assumed in order to generate the demand curve, is elegant and persuasive. It is a pure example of the Walrasian method of simultaneous and mutual determination, which avoids circularity but loses causality, in contrast with the Austrian method of temporal, causal explanation. It can be argued, however, that Patinkin's critique is not decisive, despite its elegance.

First, note that the above method of generating a demand curve for money assumes the indifference curves to exist and have the normal properties. Yet, translating into modern terms, the whole essence of the problem, as recognized by all parties to the debate at the time, was precisely that without some specific value of money *no* such indifference curves could even *exist*. Consider: we have goods on one axis, with a given intercept (the endowment), and money on the other. But money is only money when it is a medium of exchange, that is, when it has a value (purchasing power) in terms of other goods. Then it can be valued for storage purposes and the utility curves can exist.

We might place pieces of paper with a number on them on the axis, but if they have no nonmonetary utility and no purchasing power they would have no utility. The indifference curves can only exist when we place a budget line on the graph, that is, postulate a goods-price of money, and that is precisely Mises' point. Yet there must be a *series* of such values to generate a demand (or "excess" demand) *curve*, and that is *Patinkin's* point.[46]

Now, ignoring Austrian objections to indifference curves, the two viewpoints can be clearly contrasted. Mises would argue that since the indifference curves cannot exist until the budget line does, the latter is logically prior. His interpretation of such a graph would be that the budget used is yesterday's exchange value of money, while the indifference curves embody today's subjective valuations of money. Patinkin would respond (I presume) that no such particular value generates a demand (or excess demand) *function*.[47] The individual can simply postulate *various* values of money and the demands associated, and in fact this is very simple if the marginal calculus is actually in real terms. This yields demand functions, and the market demand and stock determine the equilibrium purchasing power of the unit, which, again, interacts with the indifference curves to determine the particular amounts demanded in the individual experiments.

Is there any basis for choosing between these two views? It can be argued to be a distinct advantage of Mises' method that the *particular* demand resulting, with which people enter the market, may *not* be the equilibrium quantity. That is, an "excess demand" may appear, motivating a change in the value of money, and in the next period, a change in the quantity demanded. In Austrian terms then, different points on the demand curve actually exist only at *different* points in time. This yields a process *through time* tending toward equilibrium *ceteris paribus*.

It may further be argued to be precisely the defect of Patinkin's method that, in contrast, it yields no such process. Where demand and excess demand functions are derived using given preferences and hypothetical alternative values of money, and the value of money determined by the market demand and supply functions determines the actual quantities demanded simultaneously, the individual is always at equilibrium. The excess demand or "real balance effects" upon which Patinkin lays such stress for determinacy in his system do not seem able to appear.[48] The solution to a simultaneous equation set *never* yields anything but equilibrium values.[49]

In summary then Mises was certainly wrong in asserting that a particular prior value of money *had* to be assumed to derive the demand for money. It can be done quite logically by the Walrasian method. But there is nothing illogical about Mises' method, and it even has certain theoretical advantages. Is the real world not one of temporal sequence, causality and continuing disequilibrium processes? Do not people by and large step into the world with it already running and use existing values of money in determining their future demands? Does Patinkin or anyone else actually believe that a paper currency introduced without a specified and guaranteed exchange ratio to some prior currency or commodity would find demand and have value established simply because people could imagine the amounts they would want if it had various purchasing powers? That at least the first two of these questions must be answered in the affirmative seems obvious to this author.

Mises and Patinkin:
the Similarities

It is easy to overstress the differences between Mises and Patinkin, and perhaps something should be said to balance the books. Beyond their pervasively disparate methodologies there are many similarities in their attitudes. Both men believed, for example, that, as Mises put it,

The objective exchange value of money is determined in the market where money is exchanged for commodities and commodities for money....[50]

61

It was in fact this perception which guided much of the work of both theorists, and they both recognized a crucial implication. To quote Patinkin:

> It must also be emphasized that, for the simple exchange economy with which we are dealing, the assumption that there is a real balance effect in the commodity markets is the *sine qua non* of monetary theory. For as we shall see below (p. 176), in the absence of this effect the absolute level of money prices in such an economy is indeterminate: that is, no market forces exist to stabilize it at a specific level.[51]

Patinkin went on to demonstrate, on the page mentioned, that the classical dichotomy does indeed leave the value of money indeterminate. This has become known as one of his crucial contributions.[52] Mises made essentially the same observation nearly half a century earlier (though he provided no rigorous demonstration), and also attributed such knowledge to Wieser

> Wieser expressly refers to the incomplete nature of the previous treatment. In his criticism of the quantity theory he argues that the law of supply and demand in its older form, the application of which to the problem of money constitutes the quantity theory, has a very inadequate content, since it gives no explanation at all of the way in which value is really determined or of its level at any given time, but confines itself without any further explanation merely to stating the direction in which value will move in consequence of variations in supply or demand;...But Wieser does not deal with the problem whose solution he himself states to be the object of his investigation,...The very objection that he raises against the old quantity theory, that it affirms nothing concerning the actual determination of value or the level at which it must be established at any time, must also be raised against his own doctrine:...[53]

To both Patinkin and Mises the problem was the same: the lack of integration of monetary and value theory, and hence of a theory of the demand for money.

Before closing this chapter an odd fact should be mentioned: The circularity problem has reappeared in identical form in another context, and in that context it has been accepted, at least by some economists, as a valid, and perhaps decisive critique of neoclassical capital theory. I am speaking, of course, of the Cambridge critique of neoclassical capital theory (really Austrian theory), in particular the assertion that one cannot measure the capital stock (in an aggregate production function) without knowing the rate of interest, which is supposed to be determined by the supply of and demand for capital.[54]

Without participating in the debate, I wish only to point out that the problem is formally identical to the Austrian circle, that if simultaneity is a valid solution in one case it also is in the second (and if not in the second, not in the first), and that at least one economist has applied Mises' solution to the capital problem without realizing it. Martin Brofenbrenner comments:

> It is difficult to share the contemporary Cambridge school concern with the indefinability of capital, or rather, with the increment of indefinability that is not shared by other economic aggregates like labor or output. All we need to argue to avoid circular reasoning is that the capitalization factor at time t is either the (known) prior interest rate r_{t-1} or some 'permanent' rate, such as a weighted average of several past rates $(r_{t-1}, r_{t-2}\ldots,r_{t-n})$, which determine our anticipation of what expected rates will be.[55]

Brofenbrenner notes, in a footnote, the similarity of this problem to that of the circularity problem in monetary theory, and then cites Patinkin as having clarified the issue. But clearly his own solution is essentially that of Mises, not Patinkin. It is hard to find a better example of the contrast between the influence of Mises' ideas, and economists' lack of awareness of their origin.

Notes

[1]See Helfferich, *Money*: 126-127.

[2]*Principles of Economics*: 1-50.

[3]*The Theory of Money and Credit*: 117-118.

[4]Ibid., 122.

[5]Ibid., 118.

[6]Ibid., 119.

[7]Ibid., 130.

[8]Ibid., 141.

[9]Ibid., 142.

[10]Ibid., 131-132.

[11]A modern view of the dependence of current demand for fiat currencies on their past value as commodity claims, and the effect this has had on international institutions and monetary policies is given by Lance Girton and Don Roper, "The Evolution of Exchange Rate Policy," in Bluford H. Putnam and D. Sykes Wilford, eds., *The Monetary Approach to International Adjustment* (New York: Praeger, 1979): 215-228.

[12]Lawrence S. Moss, "The Monetary Economics of Ludwig von Mises," in Lawrence S. Moss, ed., *The Economics of Ludwig von Mises* (Kansas City: Sheed and Ward, 1976): 120.

[13]*Money, Interest and Prices*: 79. That this criticism is aimed directly at Mises is indicated by a quotation and footnote on that page.

[14]See particularly *The Theory of Money and Credit*: 118, second paragraph, and note that Mises does *not* say that money has *no* utility other than that in exchange, but only that all other uses are dependent on it having exchange value. Of course even if my interpretation of Mises' argument is correct, he still may be wrong.

[15]Ibid., 157. *Theorie des Geldes*: 146.

[16]Ibid., 159. *Theorie des Geldes*: 149.

[17]This is also the conclusion of Murray Rothbard, who studied under Mises and knew him well. See Murray N. Rothbard, "The Austrian Theory of Money," in Edwin G. Dolan, ed., *The Foundations of Modern Austrian Economics* (Kansas City: Sheed and Ward, 1976): 170.

[18]*German Monetary Theory*: 163.

[19]*The Economics of Ludwig von Mises*: 32.

[20]*The Theory of Money and Credit*: 161-163.

[21]Ibid., 164.

[22]*German Monetary Theory*: 164.

[23]*The Economics of Ludwig von Mises*: 32. Moss must mean that doubling nominal balances would halve the utility of the monetary unit after prices have doubled (though he does not say so). Otherwise his statement is incorrect.

[24]*The Theory of Money and Credit*: 154. *Theorie des Geldes*: 142-143.

[25]*Money, Interest and Prices*: 24-50.

[26]*The Theory of Money and Credit*: 101-102.

[27]Ibid., 174.

[28]Ibid., 170.

[29]*Human Action*: 249, 105-106.

[30]*The Economics of Ludwig von Mises*: 44, ftn. 24.

[31]Ibid., 44-45, ftn. 23 and ftn. 24.

[32]*The Theory of Money and Credit*: 171. There is certainly empirical justification for ignoring interest rates. Estimates of the elasticity of the demand for money with respect to short-run interest rates tend to yield small values (in the range from .07 to .2). See John T. Boorman, "The Evidence on the Demand for Money: Theoretical Formulations and Empirical Results," in Thomas M. Havrilesky and John T. Boorman, eds., *Current Issues in Monetary Theory and Policy*, 1st ed., (Arlington Heights, Ill.,: AHM, 1976): 332. In the long-run interest rates have almost no effect. H.R. Heller compared the elasticity of the demand for money with respect to long-run rates (using 60-90 day commercial paper) in separate equations. The long-run rates were unimportant in all equations used. See H.R. Heller, "The Demand for Money—the Evidence from the Short Run Data," *Quarterly Journal of Economics* 79 (May 1965): 297.

[33]*The Theory of Money and Credit*: 384. Mises was being influenced at this time by Frank Fetter, who was developing a pure time-preference theory of interest. Since Mises came to see interest as a matter of time preferences, and cash balances as a matter of uncertainty, he thought changes in the interest rate primarily affected the structure of production, not cash balances, by altering the relative price of present and future goods (see chapter 6). Fetter's papers have recently been collected in Murray N. Rothbard, ed., *Capital, Interest and Rent: Essays in the Theory of Distribution* (Kansas City: Sheed, Andrews and McMeel, 1976).

[34]See below, chapter 5.

[35]Probably the best treatment of Mises' position in the history of monetary theory regarding the stock demand for money is by J.C. Gilbert, "The Demand for Money: the Development of an Economic Concept," *Journal of Political Economy* 61 (April 1953): 144-159. Patinkin, Ellis and Moss are also respectful in their treatment of Mises' contributions, and I do not mean to give the impression that they are not.

[36]William A. Scott, *Money and Banking* (New York: Henry Holt and Co., 1926): 54-55.

[37]Murray N. Rothbard, *Man, Economy and State* (Los Angeles: Nash Publishing Co., 1962): 231-237.

[38]Benjamin M. Anderson, *The Value of Money* (New York: Macmillan, 1917): 100-104.

[39]*German Monetary Theory*: 81.

[40]*The Value of Money*: 126.

[41]*Human Action*: 408-410.

[42]Gilbert, "The Demand for Money: the Development of an Economic Concept": 149.

[43]This is also Rothbard's response, and he cites the Rentenmark, introduced after the 1923 collapse of the German currency. See *The Foundations of Modern Austrian Economics*: 170.

[44]*Money, Interest and Prices*: 115-116.

[45]In order to generate such a series of values we must shift the budget line *through* the indifference curves. A strange thing happens, however, when we begin shifting the budget line: the indifference curves also shift. Suppose we start with a high goods price of money. There then would exist indifference curves constructed on the assumption that one can trade off real balances against consumption by acquiring or giving up the required number of units *at that purchasing power each*, in order to stay at the given level of utility, and one such curve would be tangent to the budget line.

Now suppose a different goods-price of money to exist instead, say ten percent lower. If these two budget lines are alternative hypothetical equilibrium states such that the money supply has also increased ten percent and real balances are unchanged, the original indifference curve must now have a tangency with the new budget line where ten percent more nominal money and the same quantity of real goods are demanded, precisely because the utility actually pertains to *real* balances.

Now at first glance a simple way out of this would seem to be to place real units of value or amounts of purchasing power on the axis, rather than nominal units of money. Some such reasoning is implicit in the Cambridge view (and is probably why they never saw the circularity problem), and explicit in Patinkin's argument. However, a "unit of real value" or purchasing power, which may be defined as the ability to acquire a certain quantity of real goods in exchange, *always* implies and is embodied in some exchange ratio between some*thing* (whether gold, some other money commodity, or a fiat currency) and goods. Treatment in real terms *in itself* does *not* allow escape from the necessity for the monetary unit to have a prior value before people can know how much they want to hold. It merely evades and ignores the issue.

[47]An assertion that Mises' method cannot yield a demand function is not quite correct. True, assuming that individual's subjective valuations of money are derived using some *particular* prior value of money yields only a single point or "quantity demanded" on such a curve, but there is an infinite number of such possible prior values, and if their tangencies with individual's existing indifference curves were plotted, demand functions of the normal shapes would result.

[48]Of course we can postulate that a change in preferences (or shift in the money stock) occurs such that the utility maximizing tangency differs from the amounts of goods and money actually held. But that immediately removes simultaneity and induces the precise dynamic process just attributed to Mises' method: The preexisting value of money is being used to determine a present quantity demanded which differs from the existing real stock, causing the value of money to change, and the new demand curve is revealed only as a set of quantities demanded at different times as that value changes, until the new equilibrium is reached, *ceteris paribus*.

[49]See the comments of F. Zeuthen delivered at the 16th European Econometric society meeting, printed in *Econometrica* 22 (April 1955):

[50]*The Theory of Money and Credit*: 141.

[51]*Money, Interest and Prices*: 21.

[52]See Mark Blaug, *Economic Theory in Retrospect*: chapter 5.

[53]*The Theory of Money and Credit*: 138-139 (see also, on this subject, 140-141). *Theorie des Geldes*: 123-124.

[54]Mark Blaug, *The Cambridge Revolution: Success or Failure?* (London: The Institute of Economic Affairs, 1974): 5-19.

[55]Martin Brofenbrenner, *Income Distribution Theory* (Chicago: Aldine Publishing Co., 1971): 398-399.

4
THE VALUE OF MONEY AND
EXCHANGE RATES

Introduction

The purpose of this chapter is to demonstrate that Mises' early economic writings contain virtually all of the elements of the modern Monetary Approach to International Adjustment (MAIA). While the essentials of the MAIA can be traced back at least to David Hume, they have at times been forgotten or overshadowed by other views. This happened in the last quarter of the 19th century, and though the monetary view was revived at the time of the German hyperinflation (1918-1923), it disappeared again in the 1930s when the elasticity and absorption approaches became prominent.[1]

Mises not only helped revive the monetary approach after the turn of the century, but was one of the earliest to cast it in modern stock demand and supply form. He also added at least one other crucial element to the theory. In order to place his contributions in context it may help to begin with a summary of the modern MAIA, which is just over a decade old, then briefly discuss its previous incarnations and development. In the process, the assumptions of the principle opposition approach, the balance of payments theory, will also be discussed.

The Monetary Approach to
International Adjustment

The essence of the modern MAIA is easy to state. The theory says that the balance of payments and currency exchange rate changes are essentially monetary phenomena equilibrating the stock demands for and supplies of national currencies. In the case of a regime in which exchange rates are fixed, either because currencies are convertible into a common commodity or by sales and purchases by central banks (as under the Bretton Woods system), deficits and surpluses are expenditure flows associated with and tending to correct disequilibria in the demand for and supply of money. To quote Harry Johnson:

> Deficits and surpluses represent phases of stock adjustment in the money market and not equilibrium flows, and should not be treated within a framework that treats them as equilibrium phenomena.[2]

A nation (say nation X) which is part of a fixed exchange rate regime cannot conduct independent monetary policy and control its price level. If the central bank of such a country (CBX) attempts to increase its money supply by open-market purchases it will increase its domestic reserves, create disequilibrium in the money market, and pressure domestic prices. Due to the pressure on domestic prices the money (MX) will flow across borders, and a deficit for X will result as other nation's central banks purchase the excess MX in order to maintain the fixed exchange rates. But the currency purchased will be returned to CBX in exchange for international reserves (gold, primarily). The loss of such reserves to CBX will offset the initial expansion of domestic reserves. This will cause MX to contract, relieving its excess supply, removing the pressure on domestic prices and ending the deficit in the balance of payments. Equilibrium will thus be restored unless CBX continues open-market purchases.[3]

In the case of flexible exchange rates independent monetary policies *can* be conducted, and changes in such market-determined rates act, along with changes in domestic prices, to alter the *real* value of money stocks until they equal real balances demanded. MAIA theorists further argue that, in equilibrium the exchange rate between two currencies will equal the ratio of their purchasing powers. This important assumption is known as the absolute Purchasing-Power-Parity (PPP) doctrine, or sometimes the law of one price, since it says that purchasing powers are equalized by the exchange rate such that no *general* advantage can be gained by switching from one currency to the other. A corollary known as relative PPP states that the percent change in the exchange rate equals the differential inflation rate between the two currencies, or, put more simply, that the exchange rate moves with the ratio of the purchasing powers.

Several other assumptions of the MAIA should be briefly mentioned. First, the existence of a stable demand function for money is an important assumption of the MAIA. Again quoting Johnson, "A proper test of the Monetary Approach must be essentially a test of the stability of the demand for money (in Friedman's sense)."[4] Second, the MAIA is a *theory* stressing a line of causation from the determinants of national money demands and stocks to the balance of payments (BOP) and exchange rate changes. Real factors may affect the BOP and the exchange rate, but only through their effects on the demand for and supply of money.[5,6] That the MAIA is a theory delineating a particular line of causation must be stressed precisely because it is tautologically true that the BOP is the money account.[7,8]

A third point is that in the modern MAIA it is the *general* purchasing powers of currencies, not just the prices of traded goods, which are made equal in the adjustment process. The MAIA views the international system as consisting of a set of smaller open economies with efficient, integrated markets, but it does not conclude from this that only the prices of traded goods are important for equilibrium.[9]

The last point relates to expectations. In an efficient market an asset price embodies all currently available information concerning conditions affecting the future value of or returns from that asset. Modern MAIA theorists assert that exchange rates act like an asset price in such a market, in that people's expectations of the future values of national currencies, and hence of exchange rates, are embodied in the current rates.[10] They go further to explain how expectations are formed, using the recently developed Rational Expectations Hypothesis. This theory says that people's expectations are formed as if they understood the true process generating changes in the value of money, using all presently available relevant information concerning those processes (in particular, present and past monetary growth rates), such that on average their expectations accurately reflect the actual state of excess demand (positive or negative) for money.[11]

The implication of these assumptions for a flexible exchange rate regime is that the exchange rate will adjust very rapidly, *before* internal prices adjust, to appearances of excess supplies of or demands for money. Until domestic prices complete their adjustment the exchange rate will deviate from PPP, and even the relative version will only hold ex-post.

Monetary Crises and the Development of the MAIA

Monetary theory seems to respond to monetary crises, and this is particularly true of the MAIA. Thomas Humphrey has traced its development through three such crises.[12] The first was the Swedish Bullionist controversy which erupted in 1745 when Sweden suspended convertibility of the Mark and its internal and external value began steadily failing. The Cap party interpreted these phenomena in monetary terms, blaming the depreciation on overissuance of notes by the Ricksbank. The Hat party argued that real factors causing an adverse balance of trade were responsible for the external depreciation, making imports more expensive, which raised the domestic price level. This latter view has since been known as the balance of payments theory.[13]

The same arguments recurred in the English Bullionist controversy. This began about 1797 when the English currency began depreciating externally and internally following the suspension of convertibility during the Napoleonic Wars. Ricardo and the Bullionists, using explicit PPP reasoning, argued that the depreciation was a purely monetary phenomenon. They denied the arguments of their opponents that real shocks such as crop failures operated through the balance of payments to raise the exchange rate. In the Bullionist view, as with modern MAIA theorists, real factors could only affect the exchange rate through monetary channels.[14]

The third controversy was that over the German hyperinflation which began in 1918. The balance of payments school, which had long been dominant on the continent, blamed the rise in the price of foreign exchange on Germany's chronic deficit. The deficit was blamed on the reparations payments forced on Germany by the allies, and on a "fixed need for imports" coupled with an alleged inability to export on Germany's part. As in the earlier controversies it was argued that domestic inflation was a consequence of the external depreciation. German balance of payments theorists went further, however, and argued that the domestic monetary expansion simply accommodated the need for money thus created. [15]

Much of the credit for the reemergence of the monetary approach at this time is given by western economists to Gustav Cassel. [16] Cassel began propagating the PPP doctrine in 1916, giving it that name for the first time. [17] When the Mark depreciation became serious shortly thereafter, he used the theory to make a vigorous attack on the balance of payments theory. Real shocks could not for long cause the exchange rate to deviate from PPP, he argued, because the opportunities for commodity arbitrage thus created would result in the rate being bid back to that point. It followed, he argued, that excess money supplies were always the cause of external currency depreciation. [18]

On very perceptive "real balance" terms Cassel denied that external depreciation caused domestic inflation. Such depreciation away from PPP would raise import prices, he admitted, but if the (nominal) money supply was constant, a rise in particular prices would be offset by a fall in others, leaving the price level unchanged. [19] Cassel was also consistent and modern on the point that equilibrium rests on *general* internal prices. [20]

Mises and Purchasing-Power Parity

Though overshadowed by Cassel, at least in the minds of western economists (in part because Cassel published in English), Mises was important and influential in the German inflation controversy not just because of his position in the Austrian Chamber of Commerce but for his theoretical contributions. Four years before Cassel rediscovered PPP Mises made the doctrine and its corollary concepts one of the centerpieces of *The Theory of Money and Credit*, properly attributing the doctrine to Ricardo while adding his own developments.

In his first chapter on the subject, Mises argued for one of the most stringent statements of the law of one price ever made. He assumed a closed economy using a single money, leaving the discussion of the determination of exchange rates between different monies for later. Money, he argued, could be assumed to be free of the difficulties and costs of transportation due to the use of checks and clearing systems. An efficient clearing system could even allow transfers without money changing position at all. If transaction costs were not affected by the distance between the parties or between them and their money, the physical location of money could be ignored.

The locations of commodities, of course, could not be ignored, and the heart of his argument was that physically identical goods available for consumption in different locations are (frequently) not *economically* the same goods.

That is, despite being identical, one may have more of the complementary input "transportation." If so, it is because each good has a subjective value as *consumption* good where it is, and a different one as *production* good in those places to which it may be transported.[21] It follows that, in equilibrium, assuming competition, and ignoring interest charges for time in transit, the prices of physically identical commodities in different places must differ only by the costs of transportation.[22] In short, "the purchasing power of money is the same everywhere, only the commodities offered are not the same."[23] In qualification, Mises also added that local differences in the prices of such goods could result from physical and legal obstacles to the mobility of people and goods.[24]

In a rather confused (or at least confusing) discussion of Mises' argument, Ellis objected that it did not show that *objective* values were everywhere the same, but only that "utility flows per unit of purchasing power" equalized.[25] Ellis appears to interpret Mises' argument as saying that physically identical goods in different places are always different goods, which *would* be destructive of the notion that objective values tend to equalize. Such an interpretation of Mises theorem is unjustified, however. Consider a good sold in any number of locations in different directions from the factory, and at distances and elevations such that their transportation costs are the same. On Mises' assumptions it is clear that though such physically identical units are at different locations they are *economically* the same and their prices would not differ in equilibrium.[26]

Having made the case for the law of one price for a single currency, Mises proceeded to discuss the simultaneous use of different monies, exchange rates, and the balance of payments. Using simple two-currency, one-good examples, he argued that different kinds of money are exchanged in a ratio corresponding to the ratios existing between each of them and the other economic goods.[27] Later he gives a clear and general statement of absolute PPP.

> The rate of exchange is determined by the purchasing power possessed by a unit of each kind of money; it must be determined at such a level that it makes no difference whether commodities are purchased directly with the one kind of money or indirectly, through money of the other kind....[28]

He follows this with a discussion of the forces maintaining that rate. Then he says that "rates of exchange vary because the quantity of money varies and the prices of commodities vary," which not only gives a clear line of causation but constitutes a simple, if imprecise statement of relative PPP.

The Balance of Payments and the Distribution of Money

The most famous and common monetary interpretation of the international adjustment mechanism, the price-specie-flow mechanism, was first described by David Hume. Hume postulated a decline in the British money (gold) supply and argued that declining prices in England would produce an export surplus and gold inflow until British prices were again the same as elsewhere.[29] Thus Hume not only asserted PPP, but what has been termed the natural distribution of specie hypothesis, by which there is an equilibrium international allocation of the world money stock.

It is to be noted that in this example Hume asserts that the mechanism operates from divergent price levels, and that PPP does not hold until equilibrium is restored. Later in the same essay, however, Hume argued that the specie flow will operate to *prevent* significant divergences.[30] Not only Hume, but Adam Smith and David Ricardo are now interpreted as holding that

75

latter opinion. All three clearly recognized the implication that, for convertible currencies, the quantity theory only held for a closed economy, primarily the world, with Ricardo and the Bullionists adding that it also held for nations with inconvertible currencies.[31]

Since Mises gained his basic orientation on the international adjustment process from Ricardo, much of his reasoning was quintessentially classical, though he cast the theory in the modern terms of stock demand and supply analysis. Under barter, he argued, no balance of payments could arise since goods traded directly and constituted the prices of one another. But this essential fact was *not* altered by indirect exchange. Balances settled in money could appear then, but such international monetary movements were *cause* and not consequence of the balance of payments. The precious metals tended to be distributed among individuals and hence among nations in accord with their respective demands for money.[32]

> In such a position of equilibrium, the total stock of money, just like the total stocks of commodities, is distributed among individuals according to the intensity with which they are able to express their demand for it in the market. Every displacement of the forces affecting the exchange ratio between money and other economic goods brings about a corresponding change in this distribution until a new position of equilibrium is reached....[33]

To demonstrate these points Mises abstracted from political and geographic demarcations and assumed a gold standard with 100 percent reserve banking, so the world money stock was fixed. He then argued that if we look beneath the monetary veil, even in international trade, commodities are exchanged for commodities. If the state of the balance of payments were such that international movements of money were required *independent of any altered estimation of money on the part of those involved* (that is, in the absence of change in the stock demands), operations would be induced to restore equilibrium. Those *selling* goods and receiving more money than they wished to hold would rapidly spend the surplus. Those *reducing* cash balances below the desired level to make the purchases would necessarily increase sales and restrict other purchases in order to restore their cash balances.[34]

Obviously these transactions and any price changes associated (which must cancel under the stated assumptions, leaving the price index unchanged) will make the balance of payments zero for other than transient moments. It is then clear that (remembering the money stock is assumed fixed) only changes in the *demands* for money (resulting in net excess demand, positive or negative) can produce a surplus or deficit.[35] Such expenditure flows are themselves self limiting however.

> Now it follows from this that a country in which fiduciary media are not employed is never in danger of losing its stock of money to other countries. Shortage of money and superabundance of money can no more be a permanent experience for a nation than for an individual. Ultimately they are spread out uniformly among all economic agents using the same economic good as a common medium of exchange, and naturally their effects on the objective exchange value of money which bring about the adjustment between the stock of money and the demand for it are finally uniform for all economic agents....[36]

It would be difficult to find, in the economic literature of the early twentieth century, as clear a statement of the modern MAIA view that international monetary *flows* (that is, deficits and surpluses in the balance of payments) act to equilibriate the *stock* demands for and supplies of money. It would also be difficult to find such a statement that was made earlier.

The point just made deserves stress because doctrinal historians eager to reinterpret and delineate the history of the MAIA have in one sense partly distorted that history. A quotation from Keleher may illustrate.

> Most interpretations of Hume recognize his natural distribution of specie hypothesis, in which world money is distributed by means of an automatic mechanism according to the relative demands for money balances. That is, the quantity of specie in any one country is a function of real factors normally associated with the demand for money, such as the volume of transactions, population, income and productivity....[37]

Note that the second sentence qualifies the first. The first statement *needs* qualification because neither Hume nor the classical economists in general thought clearly in terms of the *stock* demand

77

for money to hold. When in the second sentence Kelaher says that the quantity of specie in a country is a function of real factors normally associated with the demand for money, he means associated by modern economists, if he is talking in stock terms. Though one can find scattered hints of an "at rest" concept of money in classical writings, they primarily thought in expenditure *flow* terms. The amount of money needed in a country was that required to circulate a given volume of goods among a given population, maintain an income flow, and so on.[38] Among classical economists only Nassau Senior had a clear and methodologically individualist stock concept of the demand for money.[39] Even among neoclassical economists only a few, perhaps only Wicksell and Marshall, had a clear and developed stock demand concept early enough that they might have preceeded Mises in a clear stock demand-expenditure flow distinction in the international monetary equilibriating mechanism.[40]

This distinction is not only crystal clear in Mises' discussion, but he proceeds in the same paragraph just quoted from to derive the implications for countries in a fixed exchange rate regime.

> Measures of economic policy which aim at increasing the quantity of money circulating in a country could be successful so far as the money circulates in other countries also, only if they brought about a displacement in relative demands for money. Nothing is finally altered in all this by the employment of fiduciary media....[41]

The point here is clear: for the nation in such an international system, barring secondary effects on the demand for money, the money stock is given exogenously and is not a policy variable. By implication prices are also exogenously determined and the quantity theory holds only for the larger world economy.

Expectations and the Exchange Rate

Current MAIA theorists appear to have been surprised to discover that economists of the 1920s such as Cassel, Hawtrey, Keynes and T. E. Gregory had developed virtually all of the essential propositions of the modern MAIA. More surprising, however, was the discovery that those economists had even anticipated current refinements concerning the effect of expectations on the exchange rate and the way in which expectations are formed.

There are still serious gaps in the doctrinal history emerging. Thomas Humphrey recently published an essay designed to correct the omission of Sir Dennis Robertson from the list of 1920's MAIA theorists in several other doctrinal essays.[42] Humphrey demonstrated that Robertson made clear statements of all major MAIA propositions regarding exchange rates, including the asset market view and rational expectations. In passing, he also noted the following:

> Robertson was not alone in endorsing the asset market view of exchange rates in the 1920s. Gustav Cassel, for example, also enunciated it. Perhaps its strongest proponent, however, was Ludwig von Mises, whose contributions to the monetary approach, like those of Robertson, have been largely overlooked....[43]

The issue that the asset market view was designed to address had apparently arisen because, when the German inflation became severe, prices began rising at rates in excess of the rates of monetary growth, and the price of foreign exchange rose even more rapidly. Both of these facts were used by balance of payments theorists as evidence against the quantity theory and the monetary explanation of exchange rates. In the 1920s Robertson, Walter Euken, Fritz Machlup, Cassel and others responded with the asset market explanation of the exchange rate, which explained the latter phenomenon while retaining monetary causality.

The 1924 edition of Mises' *Theorie des Geldes und der Umlaufsmittel* (and consequently, the English translation, *The Theory of Money and Credit*) contains an excellent statement of the asset market view of exchange rates. Thomas Humphrey notes, however, that "as early as 1919" Mises had made a clear statement of this theory.[44] The statement Humphrey quotes from is as follows:

> Price increases, which are called into existence by an increase in the quantity of money, do not appear overnight. A certain amount of time passes before they appear. The additional quantity of money enters the economy at a certain point. It is only from there, step by step, that is is dispersed. It goes first to certain individuals in the economy only and to certain branches of production. As a result, in the beginning it raised the demand for certain

79

goods and services only, not for all of them. Only later do the prices of other goods and services also rise. Foreign exchange quotations, however, are speculative rates of exchange—that is they arise out of the transactions of business people, who, in their operations, consider not only the present but also potential future developments. Thus, the depreciation of the money becomes apparent relatively soon in the foreign exchange quotations on the Bourse—long before the prices of other goods and services are effected....[45]

Mises repeated this basic view in another essay, published in 1923.

The quotations on the Bourse for foreign exchange always reflect speculative rates in the light of the currently evolving, but not yet consummated, change in the purchasing power of the monetary unit. However, the monetary depreciation, at an early state of its gradual evolution, has already had its full impact on foreign exchange rates before it is fully expressed in the prices of all domestic goods and services. This lag in commodity prices, behind the rise of the foreign exchange rates, is of limited duration. In the last analysis, the foreign exchange rates are determined by nothing more than the anticipated future purchasing power attributed to a unit of each currency....[46]

Foreign exchange rates rise because commodity prices have risen. As has already been explained, it is only because of market technicalities that this cause and effect relationship is not revealed in the early course of events as well. Under the influence of speculation, the configuration of foreign exchange rates on the Bourse forecasts anticipated future changes in commodity prices.[47]

Humphrey became aware of the presence of the asset market view in these two essays as a result of their English translation and publication in 1978. The logical conclusion from this progression is that Mises first published the view in 1919 and then added such statements to the 1923 essay and the 1924 revision of his *Theorie des Geldes*. Yet amazingly, the asset market statement in *The Theory of Money and Credit* is intact in the original edition of his *Theorie des Geldes*.

Speculation on the foreign-exchange and security markets anticipates coming variations in the exchange ratios between the different kind of money at a time when the variations in the value of money have by no means completed their course through the community, perhaps when they have only just begun it, but in any case before they have reached the commodities that play a decisive part in foreign trade. He would be a poor speculator who did not grasp the course of events in time and act accordingly. But as soon as the variation in the foreign exchange rates has been brought about, it reacts upon foreign trade in a peculiar manner until the prices of all goods and services have been adjusted to the new objective exchange value of money....[48]

Mises' 1923 essay also contains another statement which is of some doctrinal significance:

> People believe that a low exchange rate for the mark is a reflection of an unfavorable judgement as to the political and economic situation in Germany. They do not understand that monetary value is effected only by changes in the demand for, and quantity of, money and the prevailing opinion with respect to expected changes in that relationship, including those produced by governmental monetary policies....[49]

Note that this quotation not only contains a clear statement of the MAIA view that all factors affecting the exchange rate operate through the demand for and stock of money, but an essentially rational expectations view of expectations formation. This view apparently occurred to several theorists almost simultaneously. Robertson wrote in 1922 that "the actual rate of exchange is largely governed by the *expected* behavior of the country's monetary authority."[50] Melchior Palyi, Fritz Machlup, Cassel and others made similar statements.[51]

Mises not only used expectations to explain disparities in external and internal depreciation rates during the hyperinflation, but also to explain another phenomenon which appeared and became somewhat chronic. This was a literal shortage of money. Such a shortage seemed paradoxical in light of the rapid monetary growth, and was used by opponents of the monetary view as evidence that German monetary policy was simply accommodative. To Mises, however, the phenomenon of an excess demand for money arose because prices began to rise in accord with *expected* rather than actual note issue.[52] American inflation has not yet (in this century) reached the proportions required for such a phenomenon to appear, but it would be interesting to see whether modern theorists would arrive at a similar explanation.

81

Mises' critique of the balance of payments approach, which is contained in his 1919 and 1923 essays and in the 1924 and subsequent editions of *The Theory of Money and Credit*, is as trenchant and biting as Cassel's. He viewed as superficial the notion that the momentary balance of payments, by dictating conditions of demand and supply between currencies, determined exchange rates. The state of imports and exports depended on *prices*, he argued, and such exchanges were carried out until price differences disappeared. Exchange rates between currencies adjusted to PPP and deviations from that rate would be arbitraged away due to the resulting profit opportunities presented.[53]

Mises denied the assertions of balance of payments theorists that, since Austria was importing 'necessities' and demand was inelastic, the price of foreign exchange could rise continuously without exports being brought into balance with imports. However strong the desire of Austrians for foreign goods, he argued, they could only get them if they could pay for them. In the absence of an increase in the money supply, if they wished to import more they had to export more. If they could not export manufactured goods they had to export capital. Since they must sell more to buy more the price of exports must fall in order for the prices of imports to rise, and there could be no *general* rise in prices.[54]

In this argument Mises appears to have assumed not only that the money supply is unchanged, but the demand also. In those terms his argument is almost identical to Cassel's denial that external depreciation caused inflation. Mises went on to relax the assumption of a fixed money stock and argued that the only reason Austrians *had* been able to increase imports without increasing exports, and that the external currency depreciation had not made imports and exports equal, was monetary expansion.

While Mises certainly had much of the essence of the matter in this last argument, it is incomplete and misses some important points. First, continuous exchange rate adjustment *can* equilibrate foreign exchange transactions even in the face of continuous monetary expansion. This is highly likely since such *ongoing* expansion could soon be accurately anticipated. Second, even if such ongoing monetary expansion resulted in the price of foreign exchange being below equilibrium, it seems likely that the nominal value of the domestic and foreign currencies traded, and of the goods, services and capital purchased with them, would be identical (and the balance of payments therefore zero) *unless a central bank intervened to supply the excess demand for a given foreign currency.*[55] If this is correct then it is the *combination* of excess monetary growth and central bank intervention designed to prevent or retard exchange rate movements which causes the balance of payments to be other than zero. There is little doubt that this is what was occurring at the time, as it is now.

Mises and the Historians
of the Monetary Approach

Despite Mises' prominence in the German inflation controversy, both as theorist and policy adviser, and despite the prominence in western economic circles of several of the students from his private seminar, few western economists are aware of his contributions in the field of international monetary theory. Ellis was familiar with Mises' writings, of course, but as one who was disposed as much toward the balance of payments approach as the monetary view, he wrote rather disparagingly of Mises' contributions to the latter approach. Mises was, in Ellis' view, "even more dogmatic than Cassel," and "noteworthy only for his peculiarly doctrinaire disposition."[56] Among modern doctrinal historians of the MAIA Thomas Humphrey is thus far virtually alone in showing either awareness or appreciation of any part of Mises' contributions in this area.

[1]Speaking of the period before World War I Wicksell wrote, "The study of the rates of exchange, which at one time attracted so much practical and theoretical interest, had been almost entirely neglected by economists during the decades immediately preceeding the war." He goes on to note that the culprit may have been the almost universal adoption of the gold standard, which stabilized exchange rates to the point that economist's attention drifted to more interesting topics. See Knut Wicksell, "The Riddle of the Foreign Exchanges," *Selected Papers on Economic Theory* (Cambridge, Massachusetts: Harvard University Press, 1958): 229, originally published as "Växelkursernas Gata." *Ekonomisk Tidskrift* (1919): 87-103.

[2]Harry Johnson, "The Monetary Approach to Balance of Payments Theory," *Journal of Financial and Quantitative Analysis* 7 (March 1972): 153.

[3]This can be modeled with only four equations. First, the assets matching the domestic money supply are decomposed into international and domestic reserves.

(1) $M = R + D$

Second is a quantity theory expression of the demand for money, L, where Y is domestic income, P is the price level, and K is the reciprocal of velocity.

(2) $L = KPY$

The third equation is purchasing-power-parity, where E is the price of foreign exchange and P' is the foreign price level.

(3) $E = P/P'$ so $P = EP'$

Substituting (3) into (2) the system is closed by a monetary equilibrium.

(4) $L = M$ so $KEP'Y = R + D$

By logarithmic differentiation we obtain the growth rates of these variables. Then if K is stable and E is fixed, for a given level of domestic income and world prices (making all growth rates on the left of equation (4) zero),

$$\frac{1}{D+R} \frac{dD}{dt} = -\frac{1}{D+R} \frac{dR}{dt}$$

and changes in D and R are inversely proportional. In the case of a pure floating exchange rate regime, on the other hand, the change is R is zero because the exchange rate equilibrates the system and foreign central banks do not purchase domestic currency to protect the exchange rate and trade the currency for international reserves. It follows that

$$\frac{1}{D+R} \frac{dD}{dt} = -\frac{1}{E} \frac{dE}{dt}$$

[4]Harry Johnson, "The Monetary Approach to Balance of Payments: a Non-technical Guide," *Journal of International Economics* 7 (August 1977): 263.

[5]See Michael Mussa, "A Monetary Approach to Balance of Payments Analysis," *Journal of Money, Credit and Banking* 6 (August 1974): 333-351.

[6]With only slight alteration of the equations used in note 3 above the determinants of the exchange rate can be modeled. First is the monetary equilibrium, in real terms.

(1) $L = M/P$ so $P = M/L$ and $P' = M'/L'$ where the primes again indicate foreign variables. Since on MAIA reasoning all factors affecting E do so through the demand for or stock of money, we can attach inflationary expectations, π^* to demand.

(2) $L = KY\pi^{*-\alpha}$ and $L' = K'Y'\pi^{*'1-\alpha}$

Next we need PPP.

(3) $E = P/P'$

The decomposition of M is not needed. Substituting (2) into (1) and (1) into (3) gives us

$E = P/P' = (M/M')(K'/K)(Y'/Y)(\pi^{*'}/\pi^*)\alpha$

which expresses E completely in terms of relative money stocks and demands.

[7]The tautological aspect is not trivial, however. Lance Girton and Dale Nattress have gone to great lengths to demonstrate that the balance of payments is related to equilibrium conditions in the money market just as the trade and capital accounts are related to equilibrium conditions in the goods and capital markets. They then show that the conditions of excess demand in the latter two accounts imply the condition in the money account by Walras' law, which says that the sum of the excess demands for *all* economic goods must be zero. Their point is that, instead of looking at N-1 nonmoney markets to arrive at the condition of the Nth (the balance of payments), as alternative approaches do, it is simpler and more direct to look right at the monetary equilibrium as the MAIA does. They go on to stress, however, that it is the substance of the theory which will generate controversy. See Lance Girton and Dale Nattress, "The Monetary Approach to Balance of Payments Analysis: Stocks and Flows and Walras' Law," *Intermountain Economic Review* 8 (Winter 1977): 15-17.

[8]Some authors have dismissed the monetary approach for this tautological aspect. See Marina von Neuman Whitman, "Global Monetarism and the Monetary Approach to the Balance of payments," *Brookings Papers on Economic Activity* No. 3 (1975): 491-536. The tautology here, however, is Walras' law (see note 6 above), which has more than tautological significnce. Its use indicates both a connection and a difference between the modern MAIA and the classical version. Classical theorists relied explicitly on Say's law reasoning to the effect that goods and services are ultimately paid for by goods and services, internationally as well as nationally, and saw gold flows as restoring this equilibrium following a change in the demand for or supply of money.

As is clear from Say's 1803 *Treatise on Political Economy* and Walres' 1874 *Elements of Pure Economics*, Say's law and Walras' law both begin from the same perception, that supplying and demanding are simply two aspects of the same phenomenon, and that one cannot do one without doing the other. Walras' law simply goes a step further by imputing this symmetry to *unsuccessful* attempts to supply or demand by asserting that an excess demand anywhere in an economy must be matched by excess supplies of identical value magnitude elsewhere. This is tautologically true because whatever is being offered for the commodities that are unsuccessfully being demanded must be in excess supply.

The significance of this for monetary theory is that, if there are net excess supplies (demands) in the N-1 commodity markets there must be an excess demand for (supply of) money, the Nth good. There then exist forces acting upon prices in general which, by altering the real value of the money stock, tend to equilibrate the whole system. It is upon this real balance reasoning, developed most thoroughly in recent times by Patinkin, that current monetary theory, including the MAIA, is based. It is clear, however, that consistent Say's law reasoning, particularly in the sense of Say's equality, reaches the same point. On Say's law, Say's equality, and the importance of Walras' law for monetary theory, see Mark Blaug, *Economic Theory in Retrospect*: Chapter 5.

[9]See P.D. Johnson and H. Dierzkowski, "The Balance of Payments: an Analytic Exercise," *The Manchester School of Economic and Social Studies* 43 (September 1977): 653-669.

[10]See Jacob Frenkel, "The Forward Exchange Rate, Expectations and the Demand for Money: The German Hyperinflation," *American Economic Review* 65 (September 1977): 105-133.

[11]The seminal source on rational expectations is John F. Muth, "Rational Expectations and the Theory of Price Movements," *Econometrica* 29 (July 1961): 315-335. See also Robert E. Lucas, "Econometric Policy Evaluation: a Critique," suppl. to *Journal of Monetary Economics*, in Karl Brunner and Alan H. Meltzer, eds., *The Phillips Curve and Labor Markets*, Carnegie-Rochester Conference Series on Public Policy, no. 1 (New York: North-Holland, 1976): 19-46. On the implications of rational expectations for monetary policy see Thomas Sargent and Niel Wallace, "Rational Expectations, the Optimal Monetary Instrument, and the Optimal Money Supply Rule," *Journal of Political Economy* 83 (April 1975): 241-254.

[12]Thomas M. Humphrey, "The Monetary Approach to Exchange Rates: Its Historical Evolution and Role in Policy Debates," in Bluford H. Putnam and D. Sykes Wilford, eds., *The Monetary Approach to International Adjustment* (New York: Preager, 1979): 147-161.

[13]Ibid., 148-149. Humphrey's primary source is Robert V. Eagly, *The Swedish Bullionist Controversy* (Philadelphia: American Philosophical Society, 1971).

[14]Ibid., 150-153.

[15]Ibid., 154-156.

[16]Ellis Calls Cassel "the recognized leader of the inflation school of theory not only in Germany but universally." See *German Monetary Theory*: 207.

[17]Gustav Cassel, "The Present Situation in the Foreign Exchanges," *Economic Journal* 26 (March 1916): 62-65. Ellis notes that Karl Schlesinger and Alfred Lansburgh used the PPP theory almost as early as Cassel. See *German Monetary Theory*: 217, 218 for discussion and citations.

[18]Gustav Cassel, *Money and Foreign Exchange after 1914* (New York: Macmillan, 1925): 149, 164-165.

[19]Ibid., 145, 167-168.

[20]Ellis find problems with Cassel's reasoning for this proposition, however. See German Monetary Theory: 212.

[21]*The Theory of Money and Credit*: 195-196.

[22]Ibid., 196-197.

[23]Ibid., 201.

[24]Ibid., 200.

[25]*German Monetary Theory*: 224.

[26]As part of the same discussion Mises argued against the common belief that costs of living are higher in some places than in others. He asserted that people would only live in places where prices were high if they felt that the "place (location) utility" justified doing so. This argument had much to do with Ellis' assertion that Mises had only shown that utility flows per unit of purchasing power equalized. But the argument here is not different. To say that it costs more to live in one place than another is to say that prices for *the same goods* are different. Ellis simply never quite grasped that the goods being talked about were not the same.

[27]*The Theory of Money and Credit*: 207. *Theorie des Geldes*: 202.

[28]Ibid., 283. *Theorie des Geldes*: 234.

[29]David Hume, "Of the Balance of Trade," in *Essays, Moral Political, and Literary* (1752), Essay V, Part II, reprinted in W. R. Allen, ed., *International Trade Theory*: Hume to Ohlin (New York: Random House, 1965): 34.

[30]Ibid., 36.

[31]Robert E. Keleher, "Of Money and Prices: Some Historical Perspectives," in *The Monetary Approach to International Adjustment*: 25-28.

[32]*The Theory of Money and Credit*: 208.

[33]Ibid., 210. *Theorie des Geldes*: 206.

[34]Ibid., 210-211. *Theorie des Geldes*: 206-207.

[35]This argument is very precise, and clearly bridges the gap between Say's law and Walras' law, relying as it does on excess demands for money and goods. It should also be noted that Mises did not just consider goods in his Say's law reasoning, but generalized it to include international transactions in services and capital. See Ibid., 212.

[36]Ibid., 211-212. *Theorie des Geldes*: 208.

[37]"Of Money and Prices: Some Historical Perspectives," *The Monetary Approach to International Adjustment*: 22.

[38]Marshall also attributes too much to his classical and preclassical predecessors when, in a discussion of how *individuals* decide the amount of their cash balances he quotes from Petty, Cantillon and Locke on the proportions of income and wealth *nations* need in the form of money. The quotation from Locke is clearest: "One-fiftieth of wages and one-fourth of the landowner's income and one-twentieth part of the broker's yearly returns are sufficient to drive the trade of any country." Alfred Marshall, *Money, Credit and Commerce* (London: Macmillan, 1923): 47. In essence these authors were discussing the M required to make the left side of the equation of exchange balance with the right side when V, P and Q were assumed given.

[39]See Nassau W. Senior, "Three Lectures on the Value of Money," in Senior, *Selected Writings on Economics*, Reprints of Economic Classics (New York: Augustus M. Kelley, 1966), and also his "Three Lectures on the Transmission of Precious Metals from Country to Country," Ibid. (Note: the page numbers were *not* run sequentially *throughout* this volume, but were begun over for each set of lectures.)

[40]Marshall was not consistent in carrying out his monetary analysis in cash-balance

terms, and his statement of the natural distribution of specie appears more in flow terms. He wrote: "The precious metals are so distributed throughout the world that, independently of the demand for them for the purposes of hoarding and of the arts, each country has just that aggregate amount of the two metals which corresponds in value to the volume of that part of her business which the habits of her people cause her to transact by payments in coin, account being taken of the rapidity of circulation of coin, and of the absorption of some quantity of the precious metals to act as the basis of a paper currency." *Money, Credit and Commerce*: 229-230. Helfferich can be definitely excluded. He was a prominent balance of payments theorist despite his cash balance analysis. See *German Monetary Theory*: 253-255.

[41]*The Theory of Money and Credit*: 212. *Theorie des Geldes*: 208.

[42]Thomas M. Humphrey, "Monetary Approach to Exchange Rates: the Importance of Dennis H. Robertson," *Commodity Journal* (May 1981): 10-11, 14-16, originally published in the *Economic Review*, Federal Reserve Bank of Richmond (May/June 1980).

The doctrinal essays Hymphrey cites are Jacob Frenkel, "A Monetary Approach to the Exchange Rate: Doctrinal Aspects and Empirical Evidence," *Scandanavian Journal of Economics* 78 (May 1976): 200-224, John Myhrman, "Experiences of Flexible Exchange rates in Earlier Periods: Theories, Evidence and a New View," *Scandanavian Journal of Economics* 78 (May 1976): 169-196, and Lawrence Officer, *The Monetary Approach to the Balance of Payments*: A Survey, Princeton Studies in International Finance, No. 43 (Princeton: Princeton University, International Finance Section 1978).

[43]"Monetary Approach to Exchange Rates: The Importance of Dennis H. Robertson": 15. Even Humphrey, however, persists in attributing the rediscovery of PPP to Cassel. See "The Monetary Approach to Exchange Rates: Its Historical Evolution and Role in Policy Debates," *The Monetary Approach to International Adjustment*: 154, and also Thomas M. Humphrey, "The Purchasing Power Parity Doctrine," in Humphrey, *Essays on Inflation* (Richmond: The Federal Reserve Bank of Richmond, 1980): 129. John Myhrman also makes this oversight. See his "Experiences of Flexible Exchange Rates in Earlier Periods: Theories, Evidence and a New View": 177.

[44]"Monetary Approach to Exchange Rates: The Importance of Dennis H. Robertson": 15.

[45]Ludwig von Mises, "The Balance of Payments and Foreign Exchange Rates," in Percy L. Greaves, ed., *On the Manipulation of Money and Credit* (New York: Free Market Books, 1978): 51. This translation comprises only one third of the original essay, which was published as "Zahlumgsbilanz und Devisenkurse," *Mitteilungen des Verbandes Desterreichischer Banken und Bankiers* 2, No. 3-4 (1919).

[46]Ludwig von Mises, "The Stabilization of the Monetary Unit from the Viewpoint of Theory," *On the Manipulation of Money and Credit*: 28, originally published as "Die geldtheoretische Seite des Stabilisierungsproblems," *Schriften des Vereins für Sozialpolitik* (Vol 164 part 2, Munich and Leipzig: Duncker and Humblot 1923). The fact that this essay and the one discussed in the preceeding note were not translated and published in English until 1978, and that there has never been an English translation of the 1912 edition of the *Theorie des Geldes*, does much to explain the lack of awareness of Mises' contributions in this and other areas on the part of English-speaking economists.

[47]Ibid., 31.

[48]*The Theory of Money and Credit*: 245. *Theorie des Geldes*: 234.

[49]"The Stabilization of the Monetary Unit from the Viewpoint of Theory," *On the Manipulation of money and Credit*: 25.

[50]Dennis H. Robertson, *Money* (New York: Harcourt, Brace, 1922): 102.

[51]*German Monetary Theory*: Chapter 12-16.

[52]"The Stabilization of the Monetary Unit from the Viewpoint of Theory," *On the Manipulation of Money and Credit*: 8-9.

[53]Ibid., 30-31, 52-53, and *The Theory of Money and Credit*: 285.

[54]Ibid., 32-33, and *The Theory of Money and Credit*: 285.

[55]The point here is simply that at a disequilibrium price the short side of the market dominates, and as regards *effective* demand there is continuous equilibrium between sale and purchase of the currencies. However, it is true that if either domestic citizens or foreigners are drawing down or building up balances of the other's currency, imports and exports may not be equal and a balance of payments, positive or negative, can exist. Mises' methodologically-individualist analysis of international transactions provides a rationale for this occurrence, but he does not appear to be making such an argument at this point. At any rate, disequilibrium from this source is probably small. By and large, in the absence of central bank intervention, not only must the value of the currencies traded be the same, but so will the value of goods, services and capital purchased with them.

[56]*German Monetary Theory*: 215-217.

5
INFLATION AND MONETARY POLICY

Introduction

In chapter I it was noted that Mises' 1912 work contained an extensive analysis of the inflationary process. This analysis dealt not only with the consequences of excess monetary expansion (which, to Mises, *was* inflation[1]), but with its origins, that is, with monetary policy and the political economy of inflation.[2] By the early twenties, when Mises revised his book, personal observation of the German and Austrian hyperinflations had clarified and strengthened his understanding. This chapter demonstrates that his analysis of inflation is strikingly modern even today, and that it contains important and largely unrecognized contributions.

The Lagged Price Adjustment Mechanism

For Mises, the essence of the inflationary process lay not in the general rise in prices, but in the fact that, since money always enters certain people's cash balances first, spreading out from there, some prices invariably increase before others. Consequently, relative prices are altered, affecting the allocation of resources and the distribution of wealth.

> If the objective exchange value of all the stocks of money in the world could be instantaneously and in equal proportion increased or decreased, if all at once the money prices of all goods and services could rise or fall uniformly, the relative wealth of individual economic agents would not be affected. Subsequent monetary calculation would be in larger or smaller figures; that

is all. The variation in the value of money would have no other significance than that of a variation of the calendar or of weights and measures.

The social displacements that occur as consequences of variations in the value of money result solely from the circumstance that this assumption never holds good....[3]

One thing that was found to be true of the former case can be predicted of this also: if the variations in the objective exchange value of money occurred uniformly and simultaneously throughout the whole community, then such social consequences would not appear at all. The fact that these variations always occur *one after another* is the sole reason for their remarkable economic effects.[4]

Mises saw adjustment to equilibrium in this process, which may be termed the *lagged price adjustment process*, as being complete, *ceteris paribus*, only when the original price relations were restored.

He illustrated this process by an example in which he arbitrarily divided the community (which he initially assumed to be in equilibrium) into four groups: mine owners, luxury goods producers, other producers, and agriculturalists (farmers). He then assumed that a new gold discovery occurs. The mine owners, making the discovery, acquire the new money first and spend it on luxury items, the prices of which begin to rise. The luxury goods producers spend their increased incomes on other manufactured goods, and those producers begin to benefit, but they are in part regaining lost ground because the prices of the luxury items they buy have already begun to rise before the new money reaches them.

The agriculturalists, being last in line, are worst off. The prices of everything they buy have risen before the increased expenditure reaches them. When it does, and the prices of their goods rise, their relative position is restored. But the losses suffered in the interim go uncompensated, Mises pointed out. This reduced consumption on the part of those groups and individuals who have to sell their goods at low prices while paying the new higher prices for the things they buy constitutes the source of the increased consumption by those who were able to increase their expenditure before most (or any) prices had risen.[5]

This description of the inflationary process is more complex and realistic than the sort of "airplane spreading analysis" (involving miraculous equiproportional additions to cash balances) that economists all too frequently indulge in. Yet as a theory of the specific way in which money entering the economy at *certain* points begins circulating and affecting relative and absolute prices, it is one of the simplest and most straightforward possible. It simply says that the new money is transmitted from group to group and raises prices in the same sequence, first altering but ultimately *restoring* relative prices, though at a higher absolute level. In a sense it is somewhat oversimplified and mechanistic, however. This is one of the few places in which Mises did not adequately explain his theory in terms of the individual management of cash balances. Income, substitution, wealth and real balance effects all need to be considered.

Starting with a gold discovery, as Mises did in the example above, leaves the reader confused as to whether Mises was discussing a one-shot increase in the money stock, or an ongoing increase in the rate of gold production. Assume the latter occurs in a community initially at or close to equilibrium. Those members of the community first receiving the additions to their cash balances (the discoverers) find themselves with excess stocks of money (and hence excess demand for commodities) despite an increase in their stock demand for money due to a positive income effect.[6] The result of this is that the prices of commodities owned by a second group of people (who trade with the first) begin to rise. Suppose the second group is rather diverse, and its members also trade with each other. They also find themselves with excess money stocks, though of a slightly smaller magnitude due to the increase in the quantity of money they demand as they perceive that its value per unit is falling.

A third group consists of owners of other commodities, who purchase from and sell to the second group (and again to each other). As a result of the spreading price increases on the part of commodities in the second group, members of the third group find that their real incomes, money balances and wealth have been reduced. The decline in the real value of their cash balances would tend to result in an excess demand for money on the part of this group, but the declines in their real wealth and income both reduce their demand for money balances, partially offsetting the former effect.

93

Eventually the demand for this third group's commodities will increase, both directly because of the spread of money expenditure from group to group in accord with the *prior* pattern of demand, and also because, as prices of commodities in the second group rise, many members of the first and second groups will substitute, when possible, the relatively cheaper commodities of the third group. The increased demand (in combination with decreased *supply* as members of the third group demand higher prices for given quantities supplied) will raise the prices of the third group's commodities, along with their incomes, wealth, and hence their demand for money. In equilibrium their relative position will be restored.

The first two groups come into equilibrium primarily as a result of the divestment of excess monetary stocks and the increase in the quantity of money they demand as prices rise. The temporary gains in consumption made by these groups stem from the reduced consumption of the third, as rising prices reduce the real income and wealth of its members. This explanation retains the essential features of Mises' lagged price adjustment process while casting it in more modern terms.[7] In fact, nearly all of this is clearly implicit from Mises' prior discussions of the demand for money. He appears to have merely desired to simplify the discussion here, and perhaps outdid himself.[8]

Mises went on to argue that the same process can operate internationally, among nations using the same money (say, a gold standard). The citizens of a nation in which gold discoveries have raised prices and the citizens of other nations dealing directly with those of the gold exporting nation may gain from their ability to buy from other nations where the depreciation has not yet occurred. Mises believed that such a redistribution had occurred from Europe to America, Australia and South Africa, due to the gold discoveries in the latter nations early in their history.[9]

One last argument of Mises' should be mentioned in this section, as it explains an important phenomenon. Mises argued that deflation, like inflation, starts with certain groups and spreads, with consequent redistributive effects. To illustrate the point he assumed a monetary contraction originating in the banking system. He then described what follows:

The first of those who have a content themselves with lower prices than before for the commodities they sell, while they still have to pay the old higher prices for the commodities they buy, are those who are injured by the increase in the value of money. Those, however, who are the last to have to reduce the prices of the commodities they sell, and have meanwhile been able to take advantage of the fall in the prices of other things, are those who profit by the change.[10]

What is of most interest here is that this argument gives an explanation which would hold even in the absence of artificial impediments to price flexibility (from government, union, etc.), why prices show a tendency to be flexible upward but "sticky" downward. Clearly people will be quick to raise prices following monetary expansion if they realize that the first to do so gain and the last to do so lose. Likewise, they will be slow to lower prices following a monetary contraction if they realize that the first to do so lose and the last gain.

The Social Consequences of Inflation

Mises went into significant detail regarding certain specific relative price distortions and distribution effects attributable to inflation. The first he discussed concerned debtor-creditor relations. Every change in the value of money, he pointed out, alters the position originally assumed between parties to a credit transaction. Debtors are benefited by inflation and harmed by deflation; creditors are benefited by deflation and harmed by inflation.[11]

Now it seems obvious that such redistributions could not forever go unnoticed by the parties involved. Mises recognized this and went on to argue that to the extent that such changes in the value of money are forseen they influence the terms of credit transactions. If inflation is anticipated the contract rate will be higher than otherwise, since lenders will demand and borrowers will be willing to pay a rate sufficient to offset the anticipated fall in the value of money.[12] In this argument the distinction between real and nominal rates is made clear, as is the nature of the forces causing adjustment of the nominal rate with changes in the value of money. These concepts had first been developed by Irving Fisher in a book published a few years before Mises' *Theorie des Geldes*.[13] Mises had read Fisher's work, and used it in developing his own views on expectations, which will be discussed in more detail below.

Next, in a section which was added to the 1924 edition of the *Theorie des Geldes*, Mises discussed the effects of changes in the value of money on accounting. The precision of accounting is illusory, he argued, since the valuations of goods it deals with rest on estimates depending on uncertain factors. But beyond this, accounting usually neglects to consider changes in the value of money itself, which results in the calculations of profit and loss being falsified. If a fall in the value of money is ignored, ordinary bookkeeping shows apparent profits because it balances against sales receipts a cost of production calculated in money of a higher value, and because it writes items off the books at their original prices. As a result, part of what is accounted as profits is in fact capital, and if the extra profits are consumed by the entrepreneur or passed on to consumers in the form of price reductions, part of the entrepreneur's capital is unintentionally consumed.[14]

If such capital consumption were prolonged, the consequences seem obvious. Investors lose and consumers gain, but if the capital stock is reduced over time (either absolutely, or relative to the level it would otherwise have reached) the general standard of living must fall (either absolutely or relatively). In an astute observation Mises pointed out that the temporary gainers from this process need not even be domestic consumers. Capital consumption in export industries in the form of price reductions mainly benefit foreign consumers. Also, since such price reductions increase exports and the capital consumption associated is not recognized, they are often welcomed by those who favor a trade surplus.[15]

Here again we have a discussion which is highly contemporary, even in the 1980s. Economists and accountants in the United States and elsewhere have become quite worried about capital consumption as a consequence of recent inflation, and have attempted to devise accounting procedures to reduce such losses.[16] Mises did admit, however, one possible situation in which inflation might actually increase the capital stock and output. In an argument which has since become known as the "forced saving" doctrine, he pointed out that this might occur if wealth were redistributed by inflation from the poor to the rich, since the rich save and invest at higher rates. But he went on to argue that capital consumption was more likely given the effect of monetary depreciation on saving (through reduced real interest rates). [17]

Inflation, Real Wages
and Unemployment

There is one relative price distortion phenomenon which seems conspicuously absent from Mises' discussion: the effect of inflation on real wage rates, in redistributing wealth between employers and employees with consequent effects on total employment and output. Actually the discussion is not entirely missing. In a paragraph discussing the redistributions, in the lagged-price adjustment mechanism, between those whose prices rise first and those whose prices rise later, Mises remarked that (European) wage laborers used to be in the latter category. He then remarked that civil servants had the same problem until they unionized and were able thus to gain quicker response to wage demands. He seems to imply that this is what had already happened to wage laborers. [18].

While Mises did not go on at that point to make his views on the subject clear, he did so later in life, particularly in essays written in the 1950s. The content of those essays is not insignificant here because the question concerning whether inflation can reduce unemployment is an issue of continuing importance. One of his essays on the subject was published in 1958. That was a portentous year for this subject, because it is the year in which the Phillips curve was drawn and introduced into western economic circles. A few things need to be said about that event and the debate it engendered before discussing Mises' essays.

Phillips curve analysis began as an attempt by New Zealand economist A.W. Phillips to establish empirically the existence of an inverse relation between inflation rates and unemployment rates. [19] At the time the evidence seemed quite strong and an enormous theoretical and empirical literature was generated. Almost from the first it was realized that, like demand curves,

97

there were factors (productivity, profits, union action, etc.) which could shift the Phillips curve, and shift parameters were included in estimating equations. Basically, however, the curve was interpreted as a stable relation which could be used by policy makers to trade-off unemployment against inflation by altering aggregate demand through monetary and fiscal policy.[20] Few ideas in known economic history have gained academic and political influence as rapidly as the Phillips curve did.[21]

In the late 1960s, however, strong theoretical and empirical attacks began to be made on the Phillips curve. In his 1968 presidential address to the American Economic Association (AEA) Milton Friedman put forth his "natural rate" hypothesis. His argument was that, unemployment being a real variable, it should be determined by real factors, primarily relative, not absolute prices. There was therefore a *natural* rate of unemployment, essentially that rate implicit in the general equilibrium equations when they are adjusted for market imperfections.

It made little sense on this basis, to assume that inflation could permanently reduce unemployment. Doing so would require that workers be subject to "money illusion," failing to distinguish between real and nominal wages sufficiently to realize that prices were rising more rapidly than money wages, reducing their real purchasing power. This might happen temporarily, lowering unemployment below the natural rate, but workers would revise their expectations and bring pressure to begin to raise nominal wage rates and their rate of increase enough to restore and maintain the real wage, restoring the natural rate of unemployment in the process. In the long run the Phillips curve must be vertical.[22]

Even before Friedman's AEA address an implication of his hypothesis was demonstrated by Edmund Phelps, using a sophisticated model of how expectations adjust.[23] The model, known as adaptive expectations, or the "error learning" hypothesis, says that people's expectations adjust in the direction of the difference between observed and anticipated inflation rates. If the difference is positive, that is if the inflation rate is greater than anticipated, expectations will adjust upward, and vice-versa if negative. In labor markets a positive difference means that *real* wages fall (since prices are rising faster than anticipated, hence faster than wage rates) and unemployment declines (reducing the marginal product of labor, which *is* the real wage). But when expectations adjust the Phillips curve shifts out. In the long run, then, its adjustment path is vertical, as Friedman suggested,[24] and inflation cannot permanently reduce unemployment below the natural rate.

One problem with the error learning model, however, is that it is equivalent to assuming that expectations are formed by extrapolation from a weighted average of past inflation rates, with recent rates given greater weights. If this is true the monetary authorities can recreate the short-run tradeoff, keeping the unemployment rate below the natural rate by constantly increasing the inflation rate, since extrapolation of this type will systematically underestimate accelerating inflation.

This "accelerationist" argument gained significant influence in the following years precisely because the rate of inflation did increase throughout the 1970s, and the theory seemed to explain why. One contradictory occurrence was that the unemployment rate did *not* fall, but actually *increased* rather steadily. As a consequence of this, and of nagging dissatisfaction with a mechanism which systematically underestimates accelerating inflation (itself a form of irrationality), many monetary theorists have turned to the rational expectations theory described in chapter 4. Under that assumption not even accelerating inflation will produce a negatively sloped Phillips curve.[25] The problem with the rational expectations hypothesis, however, is that, taken literally, it allows no learning time, which seems hard to accept in the face of costly information.[26]

It is in the light of this intellectual history that Mises' earlier writings on this subject should be seen. In his 1958 essay, while discussing the effects of monetary expansion on employment and output, he wrote the following:

> Under the conditions of this boom, nominal wage rates which before the credit expansion were too high for the state of the market and therefore created unemployment of a part of the potential labor force are no longer too high and the unemployed can get jobs again. However, this happens only because under the changed monetary and credit conditions prices are rising or, what is the same expressed in other words, the purchasing power of the monetary unit drops. Then the same amount of nominal wages,

i.e., wage rates expressed in terms of money, means less in real wages, i.e., in terms of commodities that can be bought by the monetary unit. Inflation can cure unemployment only by curtailing the wage earner's real wages. But then the unions ask for a new increase in wages in order to keep pace with the rising cost of living and we are back where we were before, i.e., in a situation in which large scale unemployment can only be prevented by a further expansion of credit.[27]

This quotation appears to contain virtually all of the essential arguments Friedman later made on the subject in his Presidential address. The existence of a natural rate of unemployment conditioned by the state of real wages is clearly implicit, though Mises lays more stress than Friedman on a particular market imperfection (Unions) in determining that rate.[28] The existence of a short-run tradeoff between inflation and unemployment and the nonexistence of a long-run tradeoff due to some sort of expectations adjustment are both explicit elements of the argument.

The argument also seems to contain a hint of accelerationism. In another essay published even earlier, Mises even more clearly anticipated Phelps and the accelerationists.

As an inflationary policy works only as long as the yearly increments in the amount of money in circulation are increased more and more, the rise in prices and wages and the corresponding drop in purchasing power will go on at an accelerated pace. The experience of the French franc may give us a rough image of the dollar thirty or forty years from today.[29]

Modern accelerationism operates on a specific view of expectations adjustment, of course, but Mises does not specify the mode of expectations adjustment in either of these statements. It is necessary, then, to examine his views on expectations closely.

The Nature and Adjustment of Inflationary Expectations

Mises' statements on the adjustment and effects of expectations in *The Theory of Money and Credit* seem to contain two distinct and somewhat contradictory attitudes and associated mechanisms. On the one hand he argued that the adjustment of expectations to ongoing changes in purchasing power tends to be slow and incomplete.[30] This view is compatible with some form of adaptive expectations mechanism. In at least one other statement however, which was added to the 1924 edition of the *Theorie des Geldes*, he apparently argued for rapid adjustment and a rational expectations mechanism.

Mises was very clear on the neutralizing effects of correct expectations.

> An increase in the purchasing power of money is disadvantageous to the debtor and advantageous to the creditor; a decrease in its purchasing power has the contrary significance. If the parties to the contract took account of expected variations in the value of money when they exchanged present goods against future goods, these consequences would not occur. (But it is true that neither the extent nor the direction of these variations can be forseen.)[31]

> Big variations in the value of money give rise to the danger that commerce will emancipate itself from the money which is subject to state influence and choose a special money of its own. But without matters going so far as this it is still possible for all the consequences of variations in the value of money to be eliminated if the individuals engaged in economic activity clearly recognize that the purchasing power of money is sinking and act accordingly. If in all business transactions they allow for what the objective exchange value of money will probably be in the future, then all the effects on credit and commerce are finished with.... [32]

He initially states that such complete adjustment seldom occurs, however, at least in credit markets.

> Thus if the direction and extent of variations in the exchange value of money could be forseen, they would not be able to effect the relations between debtor and creditor; the coming alterations in purchasing power could be sufficiently allowed for in the original terms of the credit transaction. But since this assumption, even so far as fluctuations in credit money or fiat money relative to gold money are concerned, never holds good except in a most imperfect manner, the allowance made in debt contracts for future variations in the value of money is necessarily inadequate; while even nowadays, after the big and rapid fluctuations in the value of gold that have occurred since the outbreak of the world war, the great majority of those concerned in economic life...are completely ignorant of the fact that the value of gold is variable.... [33]

This sort of statement is in line with all of his arguments on falsified accounting, forced saving, and lagged price adjustment discussed above, as they also imply slow adjustment of expectations and some form of error learning process.

At one point Mises specifically argued that expectations are formed by watching price changes. Immediately prior to a statement of the asset market view of exchange rates (that exchange rate changes anticipate and precede the completion of internal currency depreciations and appreciations) he says that variations in the internal value of a currency do not begin to affect its external value until they begin to affect prices of goods which are already objects of international exchange (or will be, with only slight price variation).[34]

It is odd that this assertion, that anticipations begin to adjust only after a change in the value of money is observed, would be made in a context in which those anticipations and the specific price adjustment they cause are argued to race ahead of the completion of the initiating price changes. If Mises meant this only as a special case of a more general mechanism, however, he was essentially assuming some form of adaptive expectations. Indeed, such a mechanism follows naturally from his regression theorem. If people watch past price *levels* in making decisions regarding their demand for money, it seems unlikely that they do not also take account of past *rates of change* of prices in doing so. Mises can hardly have failed to notice this, or that it has implications beyond the demand for money to decisions regarding the *nominal* pricing of commodities in order to set or maintain their current *relative* prices.[35]

Before one concludes that Mises was a whole-hearted advocate of adaptive expectations, however, the following statement of his must be considered.

> Since, as we have shown, it is never possible to foresee the extent of monetary depreciation, creditors in individual cases may suffer losses and debtors make profits, in spite of the higher interest exacted. Nevertheless, in general it will not be possible for any inflationary policy, unless it takes effect suddenly and unexpectedly, to alter the relations between creditor and debtor in favor of the latter by increasing the quantity of money.[36]

Here we have what is probably the clearest and most complete statement of rational expectations extant in 1924. It says that in individual cases errors can be made, but by and large expectations will be correct and no *systematic* monetary policy, only a sudden and unforeseen one, can redistribute wealth.[37] But how can statements of rational expectations, in which they are formed by watching monetary policy (and all other relevant sources of information), and adjust rapidly, preventing redistributions, be reconciled with adaptive expectations arguments in which past price changes alone are watched, anticipations adjust slowly, and redistributions occur? Which did Mises believe?

One implication of error learning assumptions which is denied by rational expectations reasoning is accelerationism. If Mises held accelerationist views he quite likely assumed adaptive expectations. Consider the following:

> The "beneficial effects" on trade of the depreciation of money only last so long as the depreciation has not affected all commodities and services. Once the adjustment is completed, then these "beneficial effects" disappear. If it is desired to retain them permanently, continual resort must be had to fresh diminutions of the purchasing power of money. It is not enough to reduce the purchasing power of money by one set of measures only, as is erroneously assumed by numerous inflationist writers; only the progressive diminution of the value of money could permanently achieve the aims which they have in view....[38]

There is a pair of problems in this statement. The first exists because Mises appears to have two explanations for why inflation distorts relative prices; one is the lagged price adjustment as money enters and circulates through the economy, and the other is that expectations are wrong. Clearly these must in some sense be the same, but he never demonstrates how expectational adjustment would reduce or eliminate the lags and speed up the price adjustment.[39]

Second, as regards the adjustment of expectations, there is a mistake in this argument. The distinction that Mises appears to make is between a single addition to the money supply, producing a specific, one time decline in the value of money, and ongoing additions producing a steady rate of inflation. However, while the first certainly would not produce a permanent price distortion, neither would the second. Any *steady* rate of inflation will become anticipated and its relative-price effects will be offset.[40] Only *accelerating* inflation will, on error learning assumptions, chronically fool people. However, the germ of the accelerationist principle is clearly present in Mises' argument, and as I have already shown, he later made the correct distinction (essentially between *velocity* and *acceleration* of price changes), nearly two decades before Phelps and Friedman rediscovered accelerationism.[41]

Still, Mises never worked out the contradictions between his adaptive and rational expectations views, as far as I can determine. It may be that he never saw them, or was simply undecided. He may also have believed, quite sensibly, that there is an adjustment period to people's expectations, but that such periods become shorter as experience with inflation (or deflation) accumulates and people learn more about the process, until they are virtually zero and adaptive expectations become rational expectations.

Inflation and the Demand for Money

One of the more important ideas in modern monetary theory is that the expected rate of change of prices in general (inflation or deflation) enters as an independent variable into the function determining people's demands for money, and that its partial derivative has a negative sign. Put more simply, an increase in the expected rate of inflation reduces people's desired *real* balances, and an increase in the expected rate of *deflation* has the opposite effect. The reasoning is simply that the loss in purchasing power of money held during inflation is an additional cost of holding money balances, and the gain during inflation is an additional benefit.

If this idea is correct, then during the period in which the demand for money is adjusting, the price change is accelerated. If, for example, the expected rate of inflation rises due to expansive monetary policy, the perceived cost of holding money rises, causing desired balances to fall. During the adjustment period in which the demand for money is falling, the value of money will fall at a rate even higher than that mandated by the increased growth rate of the money stock.

The idea is important for two reasons. First, it can be used to

104

explain what is (to quantity theorists) an otherwise intellectually intractable phenomenon, which is that prices often rise more rapidly than the quantity of money during hyperinflation. Second, the idea is essential to what is known as the "tax on cash balances" literature, which shows, among other things, how a policy of inflation transfers purchasing power from the private to the public sector.[42]

Probably the first individual to develop the basic idea, as Ephrime Eshag notes, is Alfred Marshall, in one of his early unpublished (at the time) essays.[43] What may be a statement of the notion first appeared in a publication of one of Marshall's students, A.C. Pigou, 1917.[44] As one of the first to rigorously apply cash balance analysis, and particularly given his integration of monetary theory and value theory through the regression theorem (in which the demand for money is *based* on observation of past prices), Mises was also in a good position to see inflation as a determinant of the demand for money. In the 1924 edition of the *Theorie des Geldes* from which the English translation was made, this idea made its appearance.

> In the long run, a money which continually fell in value would have no commercial utility. It could not be used as a standard of deferred payments. For all transactions in which commodities or services were not exchanged for cash, another medium would have to be sought. In fact, a money that is continually depreciating becomes useless even for cash transactions. Everybody attempts to minimize his cash reserves, which are a source of continual loss....When commodities that are not needed at all or at least not at the moment are purchased in order to avoid the holding of notes, then the process of extrusion of the notes from use as a general medium of exchange has already begun....Once the depreciation is proceeding so rapidly that sellers have to reckon with considerable losses even if they buy again as quickly as is possible, then the position of the currency is hopeless.[45]

In the immediately following paragraphs, Mises went on to comment on the fact that the *real* money stock actually *declines* during hyperinflation, despite the enormous rise in nominal balances. He attributed this specifically to a decline in the demand for money causing inflation to exceed the rate of growth of the nominal money stock.[46]

Moss has argued that Mises made a clear error, however, when he argued, as he seems to in the first part of the quotation above, that money which depreciated at a steady rate would have no usefulness, and would be dispensed with. What actually happens when a particular higher rate of inflation comes to be anticipated, as Moss correctly argues, is that the demand for money falls until the marginal benefits of holding real money balances are once again equal to the (now higher) marginal cost. It does not fall continuously toward zero.[47]

Now there is a counterargument to this, concerning the possible dynamic instability of the demand for money, and it is one of the most crucial arguments surrounding the notion that the demand for money is inversely related to ongoing changes in its value. The question is: As a new higher rate of inflation/deflation motivates a shift in the demand for money, does the consequently *higher* rate of inflation/deflation during the adjustment period *itself* recondition expectations, such that the demand for money explodes toward infinity or zero?[48] Such evidence as exists indicates that instances of this kind of instability are rare, requiring not only extremely high but accelerating inflation (or deflation).[49]

It is certainly true that the demand for money *has* gone to zero under extreme conditions of inflation in several times and places, and it must be remembered that Mises was watching this very process in Germany when revising *The Theory of Money and Credit* in 1923. Also, the last sentence in the quotation from Mises above appears to indicate that he was in fact discussing not only high but *rising* inflation. However, Mises went on a few pages later to explain that the reason the demand for money goes to zero when inflation reaches a certain point is that the cost of using the depreciating currency rises above that of using formerly inferior substitutes, such as gold, foreign currencies, gemstones, etc. as media of exchange.[50] It does not appear then that Mises was imputing dynamic instability to the demand for money, or that he misunderstood the theory in the way that Moss asserts that he did.

Mises realized that inflation is not a purely economic phenomenon, that even when its economic nature and effects are understood, if the money supply is not endogenous there remain questions of why inflation occurs which can only be answered in *political* terms.

> If a country has a metallic standard, then the *only* measure of currency policy that it can carry out by itself is to go over to another kind of money. It is otherwise with credit money and fiat money. Here the state is able to influence the movement of the objective exchange value of money by increasing or decreasing its quantity....[51]

Mises termed monetary policy aimed at monetary expansion "inflationism" and identified several categories of inflationists. One group simply consisted of those who confuse money with wealth. However:

> Other inflationists realize very well that an increase in the quantity of money reduces the purchasing power of the monetary unit. But they endeavor to secure inflation nonetheless, *because* of its effect on the value of money; they want depreciation, because they want to favor debtors at the expense of creditors and because they want to encourage exportation and make importation difficult. Others, again, recommend depreciation for the sake of its supposed property of stimulating production and encouraging the spirit of enterprise.[52]

Such "beneficial" effects could not be maintained, he then pointed out, because of the adjustment of expectations. In fact, reduced saving and capital consumption could occur.

Another group of inflationists is aware of all of this.

> A third group of inflationists do not deny that inflation involves serious disadvantages. Nevertheless, they think that there are higher and more important aims of economic policy than a sound monetary system. They hold that although inflation may be a great evil, yet it is not the greatest evil, and that the state might under certain curcumstances find itself in a position where it would do well to oppose greater evils with the lesser evil of inflation....

Sometimes this sort of conditional inflation is supported by the argument that inflation is a kind of taxation that is advisable in certain circumstances....The assistance of inflation is invoked whenever a government is unwilling to increase taxation or unable to raise a loan; that is the truth of the matter. The next step is to inquire *why* the two usual methods of raising money for public purposes cannot or will not be employed.[53]

Why indeed: His answer is that the public will not support the level of *open* taxation required for certain programs, and hence must be deceived.

It must be observed here that the greater the total burden of taxation becomes, the harder it is to deceive public opinion as to the impossibility of placing the whole burden of taxation upon the small richer class of the community....

Who has any doubt that the belligerent peoples of Europe would have tired of war much more quickly if their governments had clearly and candidly laid before them at the time the account of their war expenditures?...

What war began, revolution continued. The socialistic or semisocialistic state needs money in order to carry on undertakings which do not pay, to support the unemployed, and to provide the people with cheap food. It dare not tell the people the truth....

A government always finds itself obliged to resort to inflationary measures when it cannot negotiate loans and dare not levy taxes, because it has reason to fear that it will forfeit approval of the policy it is following if it reveals too soon the financial and general economic consequences of that policy. Thus inflation becomes the most important psychological resource of any economic policy whose consequences have to be concealed; and so in this sense it can be called an instrument of unpopular, that is, of antidemocratic policy.[54]

But can such a policy succeed? Again Mises' answer is clear. It cannot, because of expectational adjustment and the tendency of inflation once indulged in to increase until the monetary system collapses.

Most of Mises' arguments here were not totally original. That inflation is a tax, in particular a hidden tax, is a motion which long preceded him. But Mises' understanding of expectations and of the reasons why inflation tends to accelerate gave new and clearer insight into the nature of the deception involved in inflationary policy, and to the ultimate futility of such policy.

108

Having rejected an inflationist monetary policy, a question remained for Mises to answer: What policy should the monetary authorities pursue? The two alternatives would seem to be 1) to allow the value of money to rise (a deflationary policy), or 2) to attempt to adjust the money stock such as to keep the value of money stable. Regarding the first alternative, Mises pointed out that deflation is generally unpopular. For one thing, the external currency appreciation associated with deflation tends to encourage imports and discourage exports, so businessmen oppose it. Also, where deflation results from withdrawal of notes the government loses revenue, so political authorities tend to oppose such a policy.[55]

The most important historical situation in which deflation has been seriously considered, however, is following an inflation, when the question is whether the gold standard should be reinstated at the preinflation parity. Mises rejected this policy, arguing that the redistributions attendant to the resulting fall in prices would in general *not* offset and compensate for those which occurred during the inflation.[56]

That seems to leave only 2), but Mises also rejected a policy of maintaining the value of money constant. Part of the reason for this rejection was that he did not conceive such a policy in terms of a "Friedman rule" in which monetary authorities are required to cause the money supply to grow at some set rate such as the historic rate of growth of output. Believing that shifts in the demand for money are constantly occurring, Mises argued that a policy aimed at stabilizing the exchange value of money would require constant offsetting interventions by the monetary authorities. This was unfeasible, he argued, because the quantitive effects of a given alteration in the money stock could not be known before hand, or even accurately measured ex-post.[57]

Obviously no monetary policy is left, and it was precisely Mises' position that there should be no such thing in any discretionary sense. The money stock should not be exogenous, but endogenous, in the form of a gold standard. Since the publication of the *Theorie des Geldes und der Umlaufsmittal* most economists have come to view such a position as archaic, of course, though

109

there are dissenters to the modern view, and objective comparisons of the performance of the American gold standard and post-gold standard monetary system have not been detrimental to the former.[58] In Mises' view the only real alternative to the gold standard was inflation. However debatable this assumption, his prophetic track record is hard to deny. In 1950 he wrote:

> Today a pension of one hundred dollars a month means a rather substantial allowance. What will it mean in 1980 or 1990? Today, as the Welfare Commissioner of the City of New York has shown, 52 cents can buy all the food a person needs to meet the daily caloric and protein requirements. How much will 52 cents buy in 1980?[59]

How much indeed.

[1]*The Theory of Money and Credit*: 272.

[2]In the 1912 edition the discussion of political economy consisted mostly of historical discussion of Austrian monetary policy and the forces and interests influencing it. In the 1924 revision this and other historical discussions were deleted, and, among other things, a theoretical discussion of the political economy of inflation was added.

[3]*The Theory of Money and Credit*: 237-238.

[4]Ibid., 244.

[5]Ibid., 240. *Theorie des Geldes*: 230.

[6]Strictly speaking, there are *two* methods of reducing an excess money balance. One is by divesting (spending) the excess, and the other is by reducing the sales of one's own goods and services, reducing the income flow into the cash balance. Assuming initial equilibrium, either one or both of these methods implies the emergence of an excess demand for non-money commodities exactly equal (in value terms) to the excess money stock, in accord with Walras' law.

[7]Compare, for example, Milton Friedman, "The Optimum Quantity of Money," in his *The Optimum Quantity of Money and Other Essays* (Chicago: Aldine Publishing Co., 1969): 6-7. Note that Friedman vastly simplifies his problem by assuming: 1) that the new money enters everyone's balances simultaneously, though *not* in proportion to their previous relative holdings, and 2) that *all* prices double, so that all that is left is some people with excess balances and others with inadequate balances, resulting in the obvious redistribution between the two groups. Friedman seems unwilling to deal with the more difficult problem of how money which enters the economy at *certain* points affects prices with a lag.

At least one modern economist has dealt with this problem, however. Phillip Cagan argues that inflation diminishes the ability of firms to distinguish between short-term and long-term changes in demand, motivating the firms to base prices not on demand fluctuations, but on costs, with a markup. So when monetary expansion raises the demand for final goods and services, firms respond not with price adjustment, but with output changes, passing the demand down the production structure. Raw materials and labor are price sensitive, however, and when the demand increase reaches them their prices rise. This begins to raise costs, and, through the markups, prices, passing the cost increases up the production structure. So in Cagan's model demand and price increases move in opposite directions, in contrast to Mises' model in which demand and price changes move in the same direction. See Phillip Cagan, *Persistent*

Inflation (New York: Columbia University Press, 1979): 17-21.

⁸The very existence of such a lagged price adjustment could be disputed, and would seem to rest on how rapidly new money spreads and prices are raised. However, people do not usually raise prices immediately with every increase in demand for their goods and services. They wait to see whether the increase is transient or durable. If the transmission of money between groups (such as in the discussion above) is not too rapid, so that there are significant differences between the *beginnings* of their waiting periods, then even if the new money gets from the first to the last group before the first to experience the new demand raises prices, prices of the commodities owned by the different groups would rise in sequence as Mises asserts.

If the transmission of money is rapid, so that there is little difference between the beginnings of the waiting periods, and the periods are of the same duration, prices will virtually rise together and redistributive effects will be insignificant. It can be argued, however, that the transmission of new money between the groups is probably not too rapid. As each group acquires the new money, its members experience that acquisition in the form of increased demand for their goods and services, which increases their income and accretes to their cash balances. If their demand for money does not increase, they must begin immediately spending at the same higher rate as their income if their intent is to maintain their original balances. That would make the transmission between groups virtually instantaneous. But there is a normal fluctuation in cash balances. The function of a cash balance, after all, is to be drawn up or down as required in order to allow the individual to match rates of income and expenditure flow which are (particularly in the case of businesses) *both* subject to random fluctuations. During the waiting period, while these individuals are undecided as to whether the increased demand is transitory or permanent, cash balances will be allowed to build up. What is more, when it is decided that the greater demand and income is permanent, cash balances being a normal good, the demand for money will increase, and that will also increase the amount of time before the greater income flow is passed on as a greater expenditure flow.

⁹*The Theory of Money and Credit*: 241-242.

¹⁰Ibid., 243.

¹¹Ibid., 229.

¹²Ibid., 230-231.

¹³Irving Fisher, *The Rate of Interest* (New York: Macmillan, 1907): 77-86.

¹⁴*The Theory of Money and Credit*: 234-236. Physical capital wears out, and must be amortized if the firm's capital stock is to be maintained. If the firm does not take proper account of the rising prices of new equipment during an inflationary period, depreciation quotas will be inadequate for replacement purposes. Accounting profits (revenue minus cost *including* depreciation quotas) will be larger than if such price increases *were* considered. That is what Mises meant by saying that "part of what is accounted as profits is actually capital."

¹⁵Ibid., 236.

¹⁶I do not know that Mises originated this discussion of falsified capital accounting, but he refers to his book *Nation, Staat and Wirtschaft* (Vienna: Manzsche verlags-und Universitats-Buchhandlung, 1919) in which he first made these arguments and remarks

that "a whole series of writings dealing with these questions has since appeared in Germany and Austria." Ibid., 236.

[17]Ibid., 239 and 252-253. The forced saving doctrine is often attributed to Hayek, who actually learned it from Mises. Both men correctly attributed it to the classical economists, but it was a long neglected doctrine.

[18]Ibid., 242.

[19]A. W. Phillips, "The Relation Between Unemployment and the Rate of Change of Money Wage Rates in the United Kingdom, 1861-1957," *Economica* 25 (November 1958): 283-299. As indicated by the title, the Phillips curve initially referred to the rate of wage rise, but later authors changed this to price inflation by assuming prices to be set by a fixed markup over unit labor costs.

[20]For a discussion of the ways in which Phillips curve analysis influenced policy see Thomas Humphrey, "Changing Views of the Phillips Curve," in Humphrey, *Essays on Inflation* (Richmond: The Federal Reserve Bank of Richmond, 1980): 62.

[21]One is tempted to cite the Laffer curve; but while supply side economics gained great political influence in an extremely short period of time, it has not yet gained significant academic acceptance.

[22]Milton Friedman, "The Role of Monetary Policy," *American Economic Review* 58 (March 1968): 7-11.

[23]See Edmund Phelps, "Phillips Curves, Expectations of Inflation, and Optimal Unemployment over Time," *Economica* 34 (August 1967): 254-281. Adaptive expectations was first formally modeled, to the best of my knowledge, by Phillip Cagen in "The Monetary Dynamics of Hyperinflation," Millton Friedman ed., *Studies in the Quantity Theory of Money* (Chicago: University of Chicago Press, 1956): 25-117.

[24]The argument can be modeled as follows: where π = the rate of inflation, π^* is the expected rate, and U = the unemployment rate, the short-run Phillips curve can be defined as

(1) $\pi = \alpha \pi^* + h(U)$, $0 < \alpha < 1$.

If h(U) is assumed to have a linear form, (1) becomes

(2) $\pi = \alpha \pi^* + a - bU$,

and a whole family of such curves exists, including one for each π^*, with higher curves (further from the origin) being associated with higher expected rates of inflation.

If we assume adaptive expectations, such that $\dfrac{1}{\pi^*} \dfrac{d\pi^*}{dt} = B(\pi - \pi^*)$

then in the long-run $\pi = \pi^*$ and $\dfrac{1}{\pi^*} \dfrac{d\pi^*}{dt} = 0$, which means that inflation is

correctly anticipated. If $\pi = \pi^*$ in equilibrium, and

$\pi = \alpha \pi^* + a - bU$

then $\pi - \alpha \pi^* = a - bU$,

$\pi(1 - \alpha) = a - bU$,

and (3) $\pi = \dfrac{a - bU}{1 - \alpha}$ is the equation of the long-run Phillips curve. The long-run curve

is in fact the adjustment path of the short-run curves as expectations increase (or decrease).

It is steeper than the short-run curves, since its slope, $\dfrac{d\pi}{du} = \dfrac{-b}{1 - \alpha}$.

In fact, as $\alpha \blacktriangleright 1$ the long-run curve approaches being vertical.

[25]See R.J. Gordon, "Recent Developments in the Theory of Inflation and Unemployment," *Journal of Monetary Economics* 2 (April 1976): 199-201. However, consider also the following statement by David Laidler: "It is at least as implausible to suppose that economic agents form full blown rational expectations about the inflation rate as it is to suppose that they will always engage in error learning about it, no matter what systematic errors they are thereby led into." David Laidler, "Expectations and the Phillips Trade Off: A Commentary." *Scottish Journal of Political Economy* 23 (February 1976): 66.

[26]See Anthony Santomero and John J. Seater, "The Inflation-Unemployment Trade-Off: a Critique of the Literature," *Journal of Economic Literature* 16 (June 1978): 527. This essay is particularly noteworthy as the best and most complete survey of the Phillips curve literature available, but neither here nor in any other essay mentioning the doctrinal history of accelerationism that I can find do the authors seem to have considered the possibility that these ideas might have preceded Phelps and Friedman.

[27]Ludwig von Mises, "Wages, Unemployment and Inflation," in Mises, *Planning for Freedom*, 2d enl. ed. (Chicago: Libertarian Press, 1962): 154-155. This essay was originally published in *Christian Economics*, March 4, 1958.

[28]It is important to remember, however, that Friedman did stress such imperfections. See "The Role of Monetary Policy":

[29]Ludwig von Mises, "The Economic Aspects of the Pension Problem," *Planning for Freedom*: 88, originally published in *The Commercial and Financial Chronicle*, February 23, 1950. It should be noted that these essays were not written for professional economists, but for intelligent laymen.

[30]Mises pointed out that for some thousands of years people did not even realize that the value of money could be affected by changes in its supply, and the attitude that the value of money is stable became embodied in the legal structure. *The Theory of Money and Credit*: 225-228.

[31]Ibid., 229. *Theorie des Geldes*: 242-243.

[32]Ibid., 257. This statement was added to the 1924 edition, but the quotation cited in the preceding note is identical in character.

[33]Ibid., 231.

[34]Ibid., 244-245.

[35]Note what I am *not* saying: I am *not* saying that there is a necessary temporal regression element in the determination of the demands for or supplies of non-money commodities. Mises correctly rejected that notion. Marginal units of such commodities can be ranked on value scales by their direct uses, as he argued, and have their values established by trade, *without* such exchange values previously existing. But in a money economy in which non-money commodities are all denominated in money and relative values are compared by comparing money prices, the value of money must be known *before* an individual can know what *money* price to ask for a given quantity of a given commodity he/she wishes to offer for sale. Obviously knowledge of *levels* of past prices is as vital for the individual in such decisions as is knowledge of past *rates of change* of prices. It would seem, then, that not only does the regression theorem imply adaptive

expectations, but the opposite is also the case (particularly where the expected inflation rate is assumed to affect the demand for money, as discussed below).

[36]*The Theory of Money and Credit*: 252.

[37]Compare with Santomero and Seater, "The Inflation-Unemployment Trade-Off: A Critique of the Literature": 530.

[38]*The Theory of Money and Credit*: 256.

[39]However, given the reasoning in note 8 above, doing so is not difficult. To say that expectations are correct and rational would clearly imply that the waiting period, in which firms and individuals decide whether the increased demand is temporary or permanent is zero, since they know the source and magnitude of that increased demand. The additional expenditure *entering* cash balances is immediately passed on in additional expenditure *from* cash balances. No income effect alters the demand for money because people know (on average at least) that prices will rise proportionately to the excess growth in the money stock. The money is transmitted rapidly throughout the economy and prices rise almost simultaneously, reducing the real money stock to the desired level and bringing equilibrium.

[40]Oddly, Mises recognized this clearly on the next page, in the statement cited as note 32 above.

[41]I would not want to claim that Mises was alone in anticipating Phelps and Friedman. I believe close reading of the works of Frank Knight and F. A. Hayek, among other, would reveal understanding of many of the issues. Consider the following statement by William Hutt for example: "We are now forced back to the stark truth that the elimination of wasteful idleness in productive capacity is attainable only through the continuous adjustment of prices or the continuous dilution of the money unit. But the latter is a tragically evil method of attempting to rectify discoordination due to inertias or sectionalism. For the harmful repercussions of inflation become the more serious (and force an accelerated inflation) the more successfully entrepreneurs and consumers, in the free sectors of the economy, correctly forecast monetary policy." William H. Hutt, "The Significance of Price Flexibility," in Henry Hazlitt, ed., *The Critics of Keynesian Economics* (Princeton, New Jersey: D. van Nostrand, 1960): 402-403, originally published in *South African Journal of Economics* (March 1954): 40-51.

[42]See Harry G. Johnson, "A Survey of Theories of Inflation," in Johnson, *Essays in Monetary Economics* (London: Allen and Unwin, 1967): 122-126. As Johnson shows, the tax rate is the rate of inflation and the tax base is the proportion of real income held in the form of real money balances, so the tax revenue is the product of the two. Assuming collection costs are zero, government can maximize its net revenue at that rate of inflation at which the elasticity of demand for real balances with respect to the inflation rate equals 1. For complications and qualifications see Milton Friedman, "Government Revenue from Inflation," *Journal of Political Economy* 79 (July/August 1971): 846-855.

[43]Eshag, *From Marshall to Keynes*: 6.

[44]See Pigou, "The Value of Money": 36-37. Pigou's discussion is illuminating, though unlike his mentor he does not make it clear whether he is discussing expectations of one-time changes in the value of money or of ongoing rates of change. The former do *not* alter the demand for money, but only the quantity demanded. There is no

ambiguity about the fact that Mises was discussing the latter situation.

[15]*The Theory of Money and Credit*: 258-259.

[16]Ibid., 260.

[17]Moss, "The Monetary Economics of Ludwig von Mises," in Moss, ed., *The Economics of Ludwig von Mises*: 45, n. 35.

[18]Don Patinkin has asserted the possible dynamic instability of the demand for money as seriously as anyone. See his "Price Flexibility and Full Employment," *American Economic Review* 38 (September 1948): 543-564, reprinted with corrections in *Readings in Monetary Theory* (New York: The Blakiston Co., 1951): 252-282. In particular see section 11 on dynamic analysis and policy.

[49]See Cagan, "The Monetary Dynamics of Hyperinflation," in Milton Friedman, ed., *Studies in the Quantity Theory of Money*: 64-72.

[50]Compare Mises' argument here with that of Gordon Tulloch, "Competing Monies." *Journal of Money, Credit and Banking* 7 (November 1975): 491-497.

[51]*The Theory of Money and Credit*: 250-251.

[52]Ibid., 251.

[53]Ibid., 253.

[54]Ibid., 253-255.

[55]Ibid., 263-264.

[56]Ibid., 264-268.

[57]Ibid., 268-269. Price indices were, in Mises' view, inherently and incurably, inaccurate.

[58]See, for example, Machael David Bordo, "The Classical Gold Standard: Some Lessons for Today," *The Federal Reserve Bank of St. Louis Review* (May 1981): 2-16.

[59]"The Economic Aspects of the Pension Problem," *Planning for Freedom*: 89.

6
BANKING AND THE BUSINESS CYCLE

Introduction

It would be impossible, or at least unjustifiable, to discuss the contributions of Ludwig von Mises to monetary theory without including at least some discussion of his business cycle theory. Such a chapter can be relatively short, however, as the "Austrian" theory of the business cycle is the one topic in Mises' monetary economics which has received thorough recognition and discussion in the literature, at least in its Hayekian incarnation. The discussion here will simply cover the broad outlines of the theory, comment briefly on Hayek's debates with its critics, and stress a few overlooked points. Since the theory derives from and is based on certain of Mises' views on banking, fiduciary media, and Wicksell's two-rate doctrine, it is best to begin with those topics.

Banking, Credit and Fiduciary Media

"The business of banking," Mises wrote, "falls into two distinct branches: The negotiation of credit through the loan of other people's money and the granting of credit through the issue of fiduciary media...."[1] In the first case banks are lending money they have borrowed, and the amounts lent must correspond qualitatively and quantitatively to the amounts borrowed in order for the banks to remain solvent. But this aspect of banking is trivial from the viewpoint of monetary theory, Mises argued, and only the second is important, since in that case alone is the volume of money increased.[2]

The special significance of the second type of credit transaction stems from a crucial difference between the two. When borrowed money is lent there is an opportunity cost to the lender. Real resources are given up for a time, and for this reason Mises termed this *commodity credit*. When a loan is granted creating fiduciary media, no such opportunity cost is incurred by the lender, hence such loans could be granted virtually free of charge (if minor technical and operating costs are ignored).[3] Mises termed this *circulation credit*. People accept such fiduciary media because they are perfect substitutes for other claims on money (and by "money" here he means commodity money). The banks are willing to issue them because such claims are seldom tendered (unlike claim checks or consumer goods), because they perform the same functions as, and are perfect substitutes for, the "money" they are a claim upon.[4]

Mises repeatedly stressed that the demand for credit is not really a demand for *money* (i.e., cash balances), but for consumer or capital goods.[5] But since the satisfaction of such demand by issuance of fiduciary media involves no opportunity cost by the lender, and hence does not involve freeing the physical resources for transfer to the borrower in the same way commodity credit does, the question arises how circulation credit affects that transfer. Mises' answer was that the transfer was brought about by the forced saving attendant to the monetary expansion involved in the issuance of circulation credit.[6]

Money, Interest and the Wicksellian Doctrine

If banking conditions are such that the banks can alter the money supply, the question arises as to what effect this has on the rate of interest. The question has at least two levels since there is a distinction, Mises argued, between the loan or money rate and the "equilibrium" rate or rate of return in production. The latter is essentially the difference between the current prices of capital goods and the future value of their outputs (or, as Mises and Bohm-Bawerk were both fond of putting it, the price-spreads between the stages of production). These rates are related, of course, since the demand for loans is in fact a demand for future

118

physical resources or goods. Regarding the loan rate, Mises pointed out that it would fall immediately with the expansion of fiduciary media, and the demand for credit would vary inversely (ceteris paribus).[7]

Again, Mises stressed that it was *not* the stock demand for money that varied with the interest rate. Indeed, he explicitly argued that the view that interest is "compensation for the temporary relinquishing of money" was a view of "insurpassable naivete."[8]

> That demand for money and money substitutes which determines the exchange ratio between money and other economic goods achieves expression only in the behavior of individuals when buying and selling other economic goods. Only when, say, money is being exchanged for bread is the position of the economic goods, money and commodity, in the value scales of the individual parties to the transaction worked out and used as a basis of action; and from this the precise arithmetical exchange ratio is determined. But when what is demanded is a money loan that is to be paid back in money again, then such considerations do not enter into the matter. Then only the difference in value between present goods and future goods is taken into account, and this alone has an influence on the determination of the exchange ratio, that is, on the determination of the level of the rate of interest.[9]

In Mises' view there was no *direct* connection between the rate of interest and the amount of money people wished to hold. The only connections were *indirect*, operating through the effects of monetary fluctuations on prices (the operation of the Fisher effect is one obvious example, though Mises did not mention it at this point). If some fluctuation in the demand for or stock of money caused the prices of capital and consumer goods to rise symetrically, the "equilibrium" rate would not be affected. Mises did not consider this likely, however, on the basis that the lagged-price-adjustment process initially favored entrepreneurs, resulting in forced saving.[10]

In the case of an addition to circulation credit, Mises argued that most of it would accrue as demand for physical capital goods, raising their prices relative to the value of their outputs and lowering their yields.[11] In this case the drop in the loan rate would have some initial effect in reducing the equilibrium rate, though Mises thought that the latter would not fall as far as the former. The question then becomes, is there some force or mechanism which tends to restore the equality of the two rates at the previous level? It is the classic question of interest rate neutrality.

Wicksell had already considered the problem in this form, and indeed, the initial distinction between the loan rate and the equilibrium rate was his, although he had called them the "money rate" and the "natural rate." Wicksell argued that any reduction of the loan rate below the natural rate, if continued, would cause a progressive and eventually enormous rise in prices. Further, this price rise in itself would eventually cause the banks to raise their interest rate to equality with the natural rate because it would cause a drain on gold reserves. [12]

While adopting the two rate doctrine, Mises thought there was a more fundamental mechanism by which equality was restored between the rates following credit expansion. As long as the banks were free to issue whatever quantity of fiduciary media they desired, he could not see why any price rise or associated increase in loan demand would cause them to raise the loan rate. [13] As for the gold drain, it would not apply in a fiat money system. Yet even in such a system some mechanism should logically exist for restoring equality to the two rates, and it was this general mechanism which needed to be explained. [14] In order to do so Mises added Bohm-Bawerk's capital theory to Wicksell's two-rate doctrine, and the Austrian theory of the business cycle was born.

The Austrian Theory of the Business Cycle

Since Böhm-Bawerk's *Capital and Interest*, Austrian School economists have stressed (perhaps more consistently and forcefully than other neoclassicists) three points. First, all production processes take time, particularly where capital goods are used (capital goods themselves are *produced* inputs, used *later* to help produce other goods). Second, time preference is a vital determinant of the rate of interest. Third, the interest rate regulates the *time structure* of production (i.e., its capital intensity). These elements were all explicit or implicit in Mises' explanation of the effects of *circulation* credit expansion.

> The level of the natural rate of interest is limited by the productivity of that lengthening of the period of production which is just justifiable economically and of that additional lengthening of the period of production which is just not justifiable; for the interest on the unit of capital upon whose aid the lengthening depends must always amount to less than the marginal return of the justifiable lengthening and to more than the marginal return of the unjustifiable lengthening. The period of production which is thus defined must be of such a length that exactly the whole available subsistence fund is necessary on the one hand and sufficient on the other for paying the wages of the laborers throughout the duration of the productive process.[15]

Since the interest rate is a key relative price acting as an intertemporal resource allocator, Mises argued that artificially reducing the loan rate through circulation credit expansion must misallocate resources through time. The lower rate convinces entrepreneurs that more capital intensive methods, involving longer periods of production and decreasing returns, which were not previously profitable, now are, and motivates such investments.[16]

The production structure can only be "lengthened" however, if the actual physical resources required to complete the new (and longer) projects are made available by savings. In the case of additional loans made by reducing the interest rate and issuing fiduciary media, this has not occurred. In fact, reducing the rate of interest in this fashion *reduces* real saving. In attempting to acquire the resources required, those to whom the fiduciary media were loaned will bid resources away from those engaged in shorter production processes, incidentally raising input prices (of labor and raw materials), and lowering yields in production.

The resources thus acquired, however, will be inadequate for the completion of the new projects (since they are longer, requiring more capital goods and other inputs than are available, and the resources necessary for the production of the extra capital required have not been made available by additional real saving). What is more, since the output of the new projects does not emerge and final goods production is reduced by the bidding away of factors used there into the longer investment processes, final goods' prices rise, reversing the trend toward falling yields in the later stages of production. [17]

If I interpret Mises' various discussions of the subject correctly, then two things happen at this point. First, the Fisher effect will be operating (since the prices of final goods are now rising), raising the nominal rates both in production and in the loan market, though not the second *relative* to the first. [18] However, second, those with uncompleted investment projects, who are now also experiencing higher yields due to the rise in output prices, increase their demand for loans in hope of obtaining the required additional resources. This does tend to restore equality between the loan rate and the natural rate. [19] If the banks allow this, the misallocation will be revealed, the longer investment projects will be abandoned, and all the symptoms of the crash, such as unemployed labor and capital, will result.

If the banks attempt to prevent this readjustment by additional circulation credit expansion, these processes simply accelerate for all the reasons he had elaborated in his discussion on inflation. So the banks have no choice to raise the loan rate if they wish to avoid the total collapse of the monetary system. When they do raise the loan rate and cease credit expansion, the recession occurs. [20]

The Fate of the Austrian
Trade Cycle Theory

For more than two decades following the publication of the *Theorie des Geldes und der Umlaufsmittel* (*The Theory of Money and Credit*) Mises' "Austrian" or "monetary" theory of the trade cycle gained followers and influence. By 1934 Ellis could accurately remark that "the monetary explanation now commands as substantial a following as the other school." [21] The rapid dissemination of the theory at that time was due to its development and propagation at the hands of four students of Mises' private seminar: Richard Strigl, Gottfried Haberler, Fritz Machlup, and F.A. Hayek. [22] Hayek, who began teaching at the London School of Economics, influenced noteworthy economists, particularly Lionel Robbins [23] and to a lesser extend J.R. Hicks [24] and Nicholas

Kaldor.[25]

With the emergence of the great depression, the conditions existed for a major change in economic thought. The Austrian theory faced both a challenge and an opportunity. Transplanted in England and having gained tenuous acceptance as an explanation for such phenomena, it began to compete and conflict with the emerging views of Keynes and his followers. A series of debates ensued.[26] For some years the Austrian view competed successfully, but in the revolution and mass conversion that followed the publication in 1936 of Keynes' *General Theory of Employment, Interest and Money*, the Austrian view lost the majority of its adherents to the new paradigm and disappeared from the literature.[27]

Significance of the Austrian Theory

It is difficult to argue that all change in the history of economic thought is progress. Viewpoints alter over time and theories that have been rejected at a particular time have returned to dominate at another. Keynesianism, with its spiritual and theoretical connections to the earlier undercomsumptionist views of Malthus and Sismondi (readily admitted by Keynes) is the perfect example. The Austrian theory had flaws, but its rejection may have involved throwing out the baby (its legitimate contributions) with the bathwater (its flaws).

One flaw which has become readily apparent since the recent Cambridge revolution is the weakness of Austrian capital theory itself, lying in the indefinability of the "period of production" and the difficulty of demonstrating a unique relation between the temporal length of the capital structure and the interest rate.[28] This weakness is, of course, shared by orthodox neoclassicism, since its capital theory is largely Austrian capital theory. The validity of this capital theory was, however, at issue from the beginning of the Keynesian-Austrian debate.

Possibly the clearest weakness of the monetary theory of the trade cycle lay in the inability of the Austrians to clearly demonstrate the mechanism by which the loan rate was reequated with the natural rate following their divergence due to credit expansion. What is at issue here, of course, is the long-run neutrality of money, and from both the classical and neoclassical viewpoints, such a mechanism *must* exist. However, the exact nature of this mechanism is not really clear in Mises' writings.

Hayek came closest to demonstrating a precise mechanism using arguments derived from Ricardo. Ricardo had argued, on the assumption that capital goods industries were themselves more capital intensive than most, that a rise in real wages, by having smaller effect on the costs of capital goods producers, would result in substitution of capital for labor and a reduction in the interest rate as the capital intensity of production increased.[29] Bohm-Bawerk had included this notion in his capital theory, arguing that the length of the production structure not only varied inversely with the interest rate, but directly with the real wage.[30]

Hayek argued that this "Ricardo effect" operated even if the machine producers were not more capital intensive that average. Where capital is seen as labor invested for longer periods, and the time rates of profit must be equalized within the firm by substitution and between firms by competition, a change in output prices (changing the real wage) changes the time rate of profit (interest) more on labor invested for shorter periods than on that invested for longer periods.[31] Both within and between firms, then substitutions will occur until changes in marginal products reequate the time rates of profit. The length of the production structure will change accordingly.

Hayek's argument proceeds something like this then: credit expansion reducing the loan rate results in additional net investment, primarily in longer processes, thus lengthening the production structure and *reducing* the natural rate, as Mises had argued.[32] The additional investment generates incomes and output (and consequently, more investment, in wider as well as longer processes). But longer processes, by their vary nature, generate income rapidly and output *slowly*. Therefore the additional demand generated exceeds the additional supply and causes prices to rise.[33]

The rise in prices causes the Ricardo effect to operate, *shortening* the production structure and raising the natural rate. If the loan rate does not rise at that point, investment will increase, raising the discrepancy between (aggregate) supply and demand (and hence prices) even more.[34] This is Heyek's version of Wicksell's cumulative process, and just as in Mises' version, the loan rate must rise to avoid monetary collapse.

While the Ricardo effect gave the Austrian theory more rigor and precision, it never received general acceptance. Indeed, Hayek's attenuated response to an extensive and forceful criticism of the effect by Kaldor[35] signaled the end of his debate with the Keynesians, though he did write an extended and persuasive response much later to another criticism by Hicks.[36] The validity of the Ricardo effect is still a subject of infrequent discussion.[37]

Having examined the (alleged) bathwater, something should be said about the baby, as the monetary theory of the trade cycle made contributions which were admitted even by its opponents. Mises' distinction between commodity credit and circulation credit, for example, led Keynes (somewhat indirectly) to one of his most crucial notions, that of the possible disparity between saving and investment. Quoting Keynes:

> The notion of the distinction which I have made between Savings and Investment has been gradually creeping into economic literature in quite recent years. The first author to introduce it was, according to the German authorities (and Keynes here cites Albert Hann and Joseph Schumpeter), Ludwig Mises in his *Theorie Des Geldes und der Umlaufsmittel* (1st edition, pp. 227 ff. and 411 ff.) published in 1912.[38]

And Kaldor, in another of his essays in opposition to the Austrian Theory, admitted what is really the central contention of that theory, that reduction of the loan rate below the natural rate must misallocate resources temporally.[39]

Perhaps what is most remarkable about Mises' theory is the degree of integration it achieved. If his intent in *The Theory of Money and Credit* was to fully integrate monetary theory with general economics, his business cycle theory represents the apex of that effort. Indeed, Mises' integration of monetary theory, capital theory, and business cycle theory was an act of synthesis which has seldom been equaled.

Modern economics does not appear to have achieved the same degree of integration. Whatever its contributions (and they are large), portfolio balance theory does *not* treat the interest rate as an intertemporal resource allocator. The Keynesian model is a short-run model which explicitly holds capital constant, even in those variants to which a factor market has been attached. Investment occurs, but it affects only the level of output and employment. Monetarist models are no better in this regard. Interest rate changes cause portfolio adjustments and affect expenditure, but do *not* affect the time structure of production.

The treatment of time and interest in microeconomics is not much better. When interest is explicitly discussed it *is* treated as an intertemporal price. However, in most microeconomic analysis time is either absent from the functions describing sales, production etc., or is treated as a parameter. This is particularly inexcusable in treatments of the business cycle, which by definition is a *sequence* of events *over time*. Given the crucial importance of monetary fluctuations, the interest rate, investment and capital in the cycle, *it must* be treated as a process *through time* in which the relations between those variables are elaborated. Whatever the weaknesses of the Austrian approach, it is far in advance in that regard.

[1] *The Theory of Money and Credit*: 293.

[2] Ibid., 295-296, 301.

[3] James Rock has pointed out in a private communication that there is indeed an opportunity cost if there is a reserve requirement. This is correct, and I think Mises would say that that was precisely why reserve requirements were instituted by governments. He was assuming the absence of such requirements at this point, however.

[4] *The Theory of Money and Credit*: 296-300. Despite such problems inherent in the issuance of fiduciary media as the maintenance of convertibility, Mises was *not* opposed to its use. Quite the contrary, he thought the increased issuance of fiduciary notes and demand deposits had been beneficial during the 19th century in offsetting an increased demand for money in the narrow sense (commodity money, see chapter 2), and increasing the money stock (in the broad sense). This allowed exchange to develop and output to increase without causing a rise in the value of money (deflation). The development of interbank clearing also helped to reduce the demand for money, he argued, and elimination of fiduciary media would strangle the check and clearing system. See Ibid., 333, 358-359.

As for the convertibility problem, Mises felt that as long as banks operated under competitive conditions, no single bank would be able to issue more currency than its customers needed for transactions among themselves. Transactions between customers of different banks, to whom each others notes were not "money" (gold) substitutes, would require prior conversion. Therefore excess notes would be redeemed, though Mises admitted that the correct issuance by each bank could only be found by experiment (Ibid., 361-362). Under monopoly conditions, however (either due to effective collusion on a common credit expansion policy or the existence of a single monopoly bank of issue), he argued that no natural limitation on the issuance of fiduciary media exists, and the money supply can be increased as much as desired by reducing the rate of interest on loans to the necessary level. Ibid., 344-347, 396-397.

[5] Ibid., 341.

[6] Ibid., 349.

[7] While this seems obvious to us today, it was not obvious at the turn of the century, and Mises considered this simple observation to be an important refutation of the real bills doctrine. This was the Banking School argument that if banknotes were issued against commodity bills, overissuance would be impossible. As Mises pointed out, the amount of bills offered is not invarient to the interest rate.

[8]Ibid., 392. Clearly, some variant of Keynes' liquidity preference theory was already being propagated in the German literature at the turn of the century.

[9]Ibid., 431-432.

[10]Ibid., 384-387.

[11]Ibid., 388. Mises really only says that this is a strong possibility. In other places he shows clear awareness that governments often inflate for direct expenditure, which may *not* increase the capital stock or lower the interest rate. He does not seem to have considered the Keynesian case, however, of pure fiscal borrowing, with its effect of *raising* interest rates (in the absence of a liquidity trap) and crowding out private capital investment.

[12]Knut Wicksell, "The Influence of the Rate of Interest on Prices," *Economic Journal* 18 (June 1907): 215.

[13]The Fisher effect would operate, of course, as inflation reduced the *real* rate, causing nominal interest rates to rise. But the Fisher effect would operate symmetrically on the loan rate *and* the equilibrium (natural) rate, so it would *not* cause the former to rise *relative* to the latter, restoring equality between them, which is the matter under discussion here. Mises did not point this out in either the 1912 or 1924 editions of *The Theory of Money and Credit*. He did clarify the point later, however. See his "Monetary Stabilization and Cyclical Policy" in his *On the Manipulation of Money and Credit*: 123-128, originally published as *Geldwertstabilisierung und Konjunkturpolitik* (Jena: Gustave Fisher, 1928).

[14]*The Theory of Money and Credit*: 393-396.

[15]Ibid., 399.

[16]Ibid., 399-400. Here Mises argued that such investment would be in "longer" processes. Later in life he recognized that a lower interest rate would increase the demand for all existing types of capital goods also, so capital "widening" would also occur. Murray Rothbard has shown, however, that capital widening also increases the *aggregate* length of the production structure. See *Man, Economy and State* (Los Angeles: Nash Publishing Co., 1962): 491.

[17]*The Theory of Money and Credit*: 401.

[18]Ibid., 401-402. For a clearer explanation, however, see "Monetary Stabilization and Cyclical Policy," in his *On The Manipulation of Money and Credit*: 401.

[19]*The Theory of Money and Credit*: 401.

[20]Ibid., 402. In "Monetary Stabilization and Cyclical Policy" Mises laid almost total stress on this explanation for the final abandonment of low interest policy. However, it seems obvious that once the rise in prices has restored the natural rate in production the pressures for a rise in the loan rate until it equaled that in production would be enormous and cumulative, as Hayek later argued (see below).

[21]*German Monetary Theory*: 229.

[22]Haberler's major work on the business cycle was *Prosperity and Depression* (Geneva: League of Nations, 1939). Richard Strigl wrote *Kapital und Production* (Vienna: Verlag von J. Springer, 1934). Fritz Machlup strongly defended the Austrian capital and business cycle theories against Frank Knight in "Professor Knight and the Period of Production," *Journal of Political Economy* 4 (October 1935): 577-624. Hayek's major books were *Prices and Production* (London: Routledge and Kegan Paul, 1935), and

Profits, Interest and Investment (London: Routledge and Kegan Paul, 1939).

[23]Lionel Robbins, *The Great Depression* (New York: Macmillan, 1935) was possibly the single most influential "Austrian" interpretation of the great depression published at the time.

[24]See J.R. Hicks, "Equilibrium and the Trade Cycle," *Economic Inquiry* 18 (October 1980): 523-534. This is a translation of an essay Hicks published in a German language journal in 1935 (the English version was lost at the time), and is a pure example of Austrian business cycle analysis in the 1930s. That Hicks has recurring Austrian inclinations is indicated by his recent *Capital and Time: a Neo-Austrian Theory* (Oxford: Clarendon Press, 1973), and his collaboration with W. Weber to edit *Carl Menger and the Austrian School of Economics* (Oxford: Clarendon Press, 1973).

[25]Kaldor soon switched sides, of course (see below).

[26]See in particular Hayek's exchange with Keynes himself. F.A. Hayek, "Reflections on the Pure Theory of Money of Dr. J.M. Keynes," *Economica* No. 34 (August 1931): 270-295, J.M. Keyes, "The Pure Theory of Money: a Reply to Dr. Hayek," *Economica* No. 34 (November 1931): 387-397, and Hayek, "Rejoinder to Mr. Keynes," in the same issue, pp. 398-403. See also Alvin H. Hansen and Herbert Tout, "Annual Survey of Business Cycle Theory: Investment and Saving," *Econometrica* 1 (April 1933): 119-147, F.A. Hayek, "Capital and Industrial Fluctuations," *Econometrica* 2 (April 1934): 152-167, Nicholas Kaldor, "Capital Intensity and the Trade Cycle," *Economica*, n.s. 6 (May 1939): 127-152, and note 35 below.

[27]There are, of course, qualifications to this statement. Mises' own *Human Action*, Rothbard's *Man, Economy and State* and some of Hayek's later writings discuss the theory and postdate the Keynesian revolution. But little has been added to the theory and orthodox economists have ignored these writings, with such exceptions as those noted below in note 37.

[28]See Mark Blaug, *The Cambridge Revolution: Success or Failure?* (London: Institute of Economic Affairs, 1975): 33-45 for an excellent and readable discussion of this problem. However, see also Leland B. Yeager's important and overlooked essay, "Toward Understanding Some Paradoxes in Capital Theory," *Economic Inquiry* 14 (September 1976): 313-345 for a strong defense of the Austrian theory of capital.

[29]See David Ricardo, *Principles of Political Economy and Taxation*, Everyman's Library (New York: Dutton, 1973): 25-26.

[30]The Ricardo effect was therefore implicit in the Austrian theory of the trade cycle from the first. Hayek simply recognized this and made it explicit.

[31]*Profits, Interest and Investment*: 1-14.

[32]*Prices and Production*: 50-56.

[33]*Profits, Interest and Investment*: 38-42, 52-53.

[34]Ibid., 56.

[35]Nicholas Kaldor, "Professor Hayek and the Concertina Effect," *Economica* 9 (November 1942): 359-382, and F.A. Hayek, "Comment," same issue, pp. 383-383.

[36]F.A. Hayek, "Three Elucidations of the Ricardo Effect," *Journal of Political Economy* 77 (March/April 1969): 274-285.

[37]See William Baumol, *Economic Theory and Operations Analysis* (3rd ed.; Englewood Cliffs, New Jersey: Prentice Hall, 1972): 455-457 for a partial acceptance of the

Ricardo effect. For a less favorable assessment see Blaug, *Economic Theory in Retrospect*: 574-576.

⁵⁸John Maynard Keynes, *A Treatise on Money* (New York: Harcourt, Brace and Co., 1930): 171n. Fritz Machlup has made this same point (regarding Mises' possible influence on Keynes), citing the same passage from Keynes. See Machlup, "Opening Remarks: Mises, Keynes and the Question of Influence," in *The Economics of Ludwig von Mises*: 10.

⁵⁹"Capital Intensity and the Trade Cycle": 57-60. Kaldor himself found many reasons for believing that credit expansion misallocated resources temporally. He concluded, however, in almost perverse opposition to Hayek, that such credit expansion actually *shortened* rather than lengthened the production structure. He remarks, "It appears therefore that in arguing that investments during a boom are doomed to failure because they involve the adoption of excessively roundabout methods, the Austrian theorists got hold of exactly the wrong end of the stick. (But they did get hold of a stick — which is not always realized.)"

7
SUMMARY AND CONCLUSIONS

Doctrinal Contributions of Mises'
Monetary Writings

A close study of *The Theory of Money and Credit* and others of Mises' early monetary writings reveals a significant number of important and early contributions. The central task Mises undertook in writing the *Theorie des Geldes* was the integration of monetary theory and value theory by the application of marginal utility theory to the demand for money. As a preliminary task he felt it necessary to clarify the nature of value itself, and thus the first of his contributions listed here is the ordinal utility theory he developed. It is odd but factual that none of the major, orthodox histories of utility theory list Mises among the early developers of the ordinal approach.

Before applying this approach to the stock demand for money, Mises clarified the nature and components of the money stock. He developed a definition that was inclusive of notes and deposits, and did so roughly a decade before the economists of the Cambridge School adopted that approach. This contribution also has gone largely unrecognized, though this is partly because doctrinal historians have in general neglected the historical development of the concept of the money stock.

Several prominent economists have commented on Mises' attempt to integrate monetary and value theory. Nearly all of them have been critical of the central element of his solution—the regression theorem—which says that people must know the past value of money in order to determine their present demand. Patinkin showed how marginal utility theory could be applied to the demand for money *without* supposing a *prior* value of money. Patinkin's "Walrasian" method relied on the derivation of individual and market demand *functions*, which then interact with the money stock and determine the value of money, the specific quantities individuals demand, and the marginal utility of money for each such individual *simultaneously*.

Mises' regression theorem may be more important than has been realized, however. There seems to be little doubt that, on the continent at least, the "circularity problem" (which the regression theorem solved) was an important reason for the retardation of monetary theory in the sense that the classical dichotomy existed long after the discovery of marginal utility. The failure to solve this problem had prevented the demand for money from becoming choice theoretic in the same sense as the demand for other goods. Alfred Marshall's students independently circumvented the circularity problem after Mises, but only by never seeing it.

The regression theorem, by bringing the temporal element explicitly into the demand for money, appears to gain certain advantages over the Walrasian method of simultaneous determination. For one, it easily yields a *process* of determination of the value of money. For another, it captures certain real world phenomena, such as the invariable practice of introducing new currencies at *set rates* to preexisting currencies or commodities, which would be difficult to explain otherwise. Also, by making the prior value of money a crucial element in its present demand, the regression theorem leads naturally to a theory of expectations. It is a small step from the notion that the demand for money is based on observation of the past *level* of prices, to the realization that people also consider past *rates of change* of prices in such decisions.

With the regression theorem the last obstacle to the development of a rigorous, choice theoretic, stock concept of the demand for money was removed. Mises' early use and development of the stock demand approach has been generally recognised, though much of the comment on his theory of cash holding has been critical. Most of this criticism can be seen to be invalid, however, by close reading of *The Theory of Money and Credit*. Not only is Mises' approach in accord with the modern theory, but he was extremely thorough and consistent in applying stock demand and supply analysis to the problems of monetary theory.

This thoroughness and consistency allowed Mises to anticipate every major element of the modern monetary approach to international adjustment. This is true to such an extent that Mises might justly be designated the founding father of the MAIA in the 20th century. Some economists, both Austrian and non-Austrian, are aware of Mises' early rejuvenation of the purchasing-power-parity doctrine, anticipating even Cassel who usually gets the credit. But who is aware that Mises was among the first, if not *the* first, to correctly state the *stock* demand-expenditure *flow* distinction in the hypothesis of the natural distribution of specie? Who is aware of his methodologically-individualist demonstration that a balance of payments flow stems from and tends to eliminate disequilibrium in the stock demand for and supply of money?

Again, who is aware of Mises' argument that *all* factors affecting the exchange rate operate through the demand for and stock of money, or of his *very* early statement of the asset market view of exchange rates, or that nearly all of these arguments are contained in the original 1912 edition of the *Theorie des Geldes und der Umlaufsmittel*? The answer seems to be almost no one, with the partial exception of Thomas Humphrey, who cites some of these arguments in essays Mises published in 1919 and 1923. Even current followers of Mises' seem, as of this date, to be oddly unaware of most of his contributions in this area, perhaps because the rediscovery of the MAIA is so recent, and because they have tended to focus on those elements in Mises' monetary economics which *distinguish* it from neoclassical analysis.

The modern character of Mises' monetary analysis is readily apparent in his discussion of inflation. He repeatedly stressed that what is important about inflation is its effect on *relative* prices. His lagged price adjustment mechanism clearly anticipated modern discussions of the way in which new money circulates through the economy, first distorting and later restoring relative prices. Mises' analysis of falsified accounting, originating in 1919, was seminal. Forced saving, a doctrine neglected since classical times, was a central element in Mises' explanation of the redistributions of wealth attendant to the relative price distortions associated with inflation. Outside of the Austrian

School, very few economists seem aware of these contributions.

Mises' early discussion of expectations and the effect of their adjustment is both highly modern and largely neglected. Irving Fisher was his main predecessor here, and the "Fisher effect" was no mystery to Mises. By 1924 Mises was displaying some indecision as to whether expectations were adaptive or rational, but this is the same dilemma facing current theorists. Most evidence indicates that he leaned toward the adaptive view (which, as I have argued, followed naturally from his regression theorem), perhaps with the qualification that accumulated experience with persistent price level changes shortens adjustment periods. In publications from 1912 to 1958, Mises seems to have anticipated the accelerationist and natural rate doctrines of Edmund Phelps and Milton Friedman. Doctrinal historians do not seem yet to realize that these ideas might have existed before 1967.

One of the more crucial effects of the adjustment of inflationary expectations involves alterations in the demand for money, and Mises was one of the earliest to elaborate this phenomenon and its implications. His analysis is ambiguous in spots, and has been criticized, but it is defensible. And last, as a special case of his analysis of inflation, in particular as a special case of the lagged price adjustment mechanism, one must include the monetary theory of the business cycle among Mises' important contributions. This theory achieved wide dissemination and discussion, though it may be argued that some of its crucial insights have been lost to the economics profession at large.

This list of Mises' contributions to monetary theory and related topics is anything but inclusive. Indeed, I have been quite selective in the subjects discussed here. It is an add fact that Mises' monetary economics has tended to become *more* relevant over time, rather than less so, as economic events and theoretical developments have revealed the significance of his initial insights. This process may not yet be complete.

Mises' Position in Doctrinal History

Following a casual reading of *The Theory of Money and Credit*, this study was motivated by an observation, which at the time was hardly scientific and even bordered on intuition, that Mises' contributions to monetary theory early in this century were more important and numerous than modern historians of monetary doctrines were aware of. This "intuition" suggested the more formal hypothesis used here, the definition of a contribution required by that hypothesis, and the effort to test the hypothesis by reference to the literature on monetary theory and doctrinal history.

The hypothesis is that Mises made no important contributions to monetary theory and related topics which orthodox economists have failed to recognize and credit in their special or general doctrinal histories. The claim made here is that the evidence I have presented strongly indicates that this hypothesis is false. As in any scientific study of this type, the results must be considered to some extent tenuous. I cannot claim that there does not exist *somewhere* in the literature a statement of recognition of every one of Mises' contributions identified here, because it is impossible to examine *all* of the literature. This fact itself suggests sympathy with and tolerance for doctrinal historians who, in individual cases, have overlooked Mises' contributions on the subjects they were discussing.

Nevertheless, while some of Mises' contributions to monetary theory and related topics have been given varying degrees of recognition, taken as a whole a clear pattern of neglect of his work by doctrinal historians emerges. Repeatedly, other major economists of the day are (correctly) cited, while Mises is not cited, on monetary subjects to which he made undeniable and early contributions. Inclusion in the principle doctrinal essays on such subjects is what *constitutes* adequate recognition.

In part this neglect of Mises is explained by the historically late translations of his work. The late translations also need to be explained, of course, but the cost of such translation in the United States, where few people speak any foreign language, may itself be adequate explanation. (After all, even where Mises' followers have undertaken translation of his works, this has usually occurred only after a protracted period.) There may also be something of a general, subconscious Anglo-Saxon bias against continental European economists. The repeated references to the origins of cash balance analysis in the writings of the Cambridge authors and general neglect of the Germanic authors who were in print on the subject long before their Cambridge colleagues serves as a good example.

Given Mises' laissez-faire normative views (and non-positivist methodology), it is tempting to include ideological bias among the reasons for the comparative neglect of his work. Certainly laissez-faire was not the ideological trend in his lifetime, and he seems to have been treated rather shabbily by his academic colleagues both in Vienna and the United States. (He was never able to obtain a full-time position with a full-time salary at an American university.) Such a hypothesis seems difficult to sustain, however, given the success and recognition attained by his student, F.A. Hayek, who was as strong and open an advocate of the free Market (and as nonpositivist) as was Mises. What can be sustained, and is sustained by this study, is that Mises has not been accorded the recognition he deserves in the history of monetary theory.

BIBLIOGRAPHY

BOOKS

Allen, William R., ed., *International Trade Theory: Hume to Ohlin*. New York: Random House, 1965.

Anderson, Benjamin M. *The Value of Money*. New York: Macmillan, 1917.

Baumol, William J. *Economic Theory and Operations Analysis*. 3rd ed. Englewood Cliffs, New Jersey: Prentice Hall 1972.

Bien, Bettine. *The Works of Ludwig von Mises*. New York: Foundation for Economic Education, 1970.

Black, R. D. Collison, Coats, W.W., and Goodwin, Crawford, D. W. *The Marginal Revolution in Economics*. Durham, North Carolina: Duke University Press, 1973.

Blaug, Mark. *The Cambridge Revolution: Success or Failure?* London: Institute of Economic Affairs, 1975.

_____. *Economic Theory in Retrospect*. 3rd ed., Cambridge: Cambridge University Press, 1978.

Böhm-Bawerk, Eugen. *Value and Price: an Extract from the Positive Theory of Capital*. South Holland, Illinois: The Libertarian Press, 1971.

Boorman, John T., and Havrilesky, Thomas M., eds. *Current Issues in Monetary Theory and Policy*. 1st ed. Arlington Heights, Illinois: Ahm, 1976.

Bowley, Marian. *Nassau Senior and Classical Economics*. New York: Augustus M. Kelley, 1949.

Brofenbrenner, Martin. *Income Distribution Theory*. Chicago: Aldine Publishing Co., 1971.

Cagan, Phillip. *Persistant Inflation*. New York: Columbia University Press, 1979.

Cairnes, John Elliot, *The Character and Logical Method of Political Economy*. 2d ed. London: Macmillan, 1875.

Cassel, Gustav. *Money and Foreign Exchange after 1914*. New York: Macmillan, 1925.

_____. *The Theory of Social Economy*. New York: Harcourt, Brace, 1924.

Dolan, Edwin G., ed., *The Foundations of Modern Austrian Economics*. Kansas City: Sheed and Ward, 1976.

Ellis, Howard. *German Monetary Theory, 1905-1933*. Cambridge, Massauchusetts: Harvard University Press, 1934.

Eshag, Ephrime. *From Marshall to Keynes: an Essay on the Monetary Theory of the Cambridge School*. London: Basil Blackwell, 1963.

Fetter, Frank A. *Capital, Interest and Rent: Essays in the Theory of Distribution*. Murray N. Rothbard, ed. Kansas City: Sheed, Andrews and McMeel, 1976.

Fisher, Irving. *The Purchasing Power of Money*. New York: Macmillan, 1911.

_____. *The Rate of Interest*. New York: Macmillan, 1907.

Frenkel, Jacob, and Johnson, Harry G., eds. *The Economics of Exchange Rates: Selected Studies*. Reading, Massachusetts: Addison Wesley, 1978.

Friedman, Milton. *The Methodology of Positive Economics*. Chicago: University of Chicago Press, 1953.

_____. *The Optimum Quantity of Money and Other Essays*. Chicago: Aldine Publishing Co., 1969.

_____. *Studies in the Quantity Theory of Money*. Chicago: University of Chicago Press, 1956.

Haberler, Gottfried. *Prosperity and Depression*. 3rd ed. New York: United Nations, 1946.

Hawtrey, R. G. *Currency and Credit*. London: Longmans, Green and Co., 1919.

Hayek, F. A. *The Counter Revolution of Science*. Glenco, Illinois: The Free Press, 1952.

_____. *Denationalization of Money*. London: Institute of Economic Affairs, 1976.

_____. *Individualism and Economic Order*. London: Routledge and Kegan Paul, 1952.

_____. *Prices and Production*. London: Routledge and Kegan, Paul, 1935.

_____. *Profits, Interest and Investment*. London: Routledge and Kegan Paul, 1939.

Helfferich, Karl. *Money*. London: Ernest Benn Ltd., 1927.

Hicks, J. R. and Weber, W., eds. *Carl Menger and the Austrian School of Economics*. Oxford: The Clarendon Press, 1973.

Hicks, J. R. *Value and Capital*. 2nd ed., Oxford: Oxford University Press, 1946.

Humphrey, Thomas M. *Essays on Inflation*. Richmond: The Federal Reserve Bank of Richmond, 1980.

Johnson, Harry G. *Essays in Monetary Economics*. London: Allen and Unwin, 1967.

Kaldor, Nicholas, *Essays on Economic Stability and Growth*. Glenco, Illinois: The Free Press, 1960.

Keynes, John Maynard. *A Treatise on Money*. New York: Harcourt, Brace, 1930.

Kirzner, Israel. *Competition and Entrepreneurship*. Chicago: University of Chicago Press, 1974.

Knapp, Georg Friedrich. *Stattliche Theorie des Geldes*. Leipzig: Dunker and Humblot, 1905.

Liefmann, Robert. *Geld and Gold*. Stuttgart: Deutsche Verlags-anstalt, 1916.

Marshall, Alfred. *Money, Credit and Commerce*. London: Macmillan, 1923.

Menger, Carl. *Principles of Economics*. Glenco, Illinois: The Free Press, 1950.

Mises, Ludwig von. *Geldwertstabilisierung und Konjunkturepolitik*. Jena: Gustav Fisher, 1928.

_____. *Human Action*. 3rd ed. Chicago: Henry Regnery Co., 1963.

_____. *On the Manipulation of Money and Credit*. Percy L. Greaves, ed. New York: Free Market Books, 1978.

_____. *Notes and Recollections*. South-Holland, Illinois: Libertarian Press, 1978.

_____. *Planning for Freedom*. 2d enl. ed., Chicago: Libertarian Press, 1962.

_____. *Theorie des Geldes und der Umlaufsmittel*. Munich and Leipzig: Dunker and Humblot, 1912.

_____. *The Theory of Money and Credit*. Indianapolis: Liberty Classics, 1981. (English translation of revised, 1924, ed., of *Theorie des Geldes und der Umlaufsmittel*. Trans. by H. E. Batson.) 1st English ed. London: Jonathan Cape Ltd., 1934.

Moss, Lawrence S., ed. *The Economics of Ludwig von Mises: Toward A Critical Reappraisal*. Kansas City: Sheed and Ward, 1976.

Nussbaum, Arthur. *Das Geld in Theorie und Praxis des Deutschen und ausländischen Rechts*. Tübingin: Mohr, 1925.

Patinkin, Don. *Anticipations of the General Theory?* Chicago: University of Chicago Press, 1982.

_____. *Money, Interest and Prices*. Evanston, Illinois: Row, Peterson and Co., 1956.

Popper, Karl. *The Poverty of Historicism*. London: Routledge and Kegan Paul, 1957.

Reekie, Duncan W. *Industry, Prices and Markets*. New York, Halsted Press, 1979.

Ricardo, David. *Principles of Political Economy and Taxation*. New York: Dutton, 1973.

Robbins, Lionel. *The Great Depression*. New York: Macmillan, 1935.

Robertson, Dennis H. *Money*. New York: Harcourt, Brace, 1922.

Rothbard, Murray N. *Man, Economy and State*. Los Angeles: Nash Publishing Co., 1962.

Schumpeter, Joseph. *History of Economic Analysis*. 4th ed. New York: Oxford University Press, 1961.

Scott, William A. *Money and Banking*. New York: Henry Holt and Co., 1926.

Senior, Nassau W. *Selected Writings on Economics*, Reprints of Economic Classics. New York: Augustus M. Kelley, 1966.

Stigler, George. *Production and Distribution Theories*. New York: Macmillan, 1946.

Strigl, Richard. *Kapital und Production*. Vienna: Verlag von J. Springer, 1934.

Toward Liberty: Essays in Honor of Ludwig von Mises on the Occasion of his 90th Birthday. Vol. I and II. Menlo Park, California: Institute for Humane Studies, 1971.

Wagemen, Ernst. *Allgemeine Geldlehre*. Berlin: H. R. Englemann, 1923.

Wicksell, Knut. *Interest and Prices*. New York: Augustus M. Kelley, 1962. (English Trans. by R. R. Kahn of *Geldzins und Guterpreise*. Jena: Gustav Fisher, 1898.)

_____. *Lectures on Political Economy*. Vol. 2 New York: Macmillan, 1935.

_____. *Selected Papers on Economic Theory*. Cambridge, Massachusetts: Harvard University Press, 1958.

ARTICLES

Allen R. D. G. "The Nature of Indifference Curves." *Review of Economic Studies* 1 (February 1933): 110-121.

_____. "A Reconsideration of the Theory of Value, Part II." *Economica*, n.s. 1 (May 1934): 196-219.

Boland, L. A. "Time in Economics vs Economics in Time." *Canadian Journal of Economics* 11 (May 1978): 242-249.

Bordo, Michael David. "The Classical Gold Standard: Some Lessons for Today." The Federal Reserve Bank of St. Louis *Review* (May 1981): 2-16.

Cagan, Phillip. "The Monetary Dynamices of Hyperinflation." Milton Friedman, ed. *Studies in the Quantity Theory of Money.* Chicago: University of Chicago Press, 1956, pp. 64-72.

Cannan, E. "The Application of the Theoretical Apparatus of Supply and Demand to Units of Currency." *Economic Journal* 31 (December 1921): 453-461.

Cassel, Gustav. "The Present Situation in the Foreign Exchanges." *Economic Journal* 26 (March 1916): 62-65.

East, John P. "American Conservative Thought: the Impact of Ludwig von Mises." *Modern Age* 23 (Fall 1979): 338-350.

Edwards, James Rolph. "Ideology, Economics and Knowledge." *Reason Papers* No. 7 (Spring 1981): 53-71.

Frenkel, Jacob. "The Forward Exchange Rate, Expectations and the Demand for Money: The German Hyperinflation." *American Economic Review* 65 (September 1977): 105-133.

_____. "A Monetary Approach to the Exchange Rate: Doctrinal Aspects and Empirical Evidence." *Scandinavian Journal of Economics* 78 (May 1976): 200-224.

Friedman, Milton. "Government Revenue from Inflation." *Journal of Political Economy* 79 (July/August 1971): 846-855.

_____. "The Role of Monetary Policy." *American Economic Review* 58 (March 1968): 1-17.

Gilbert, J.C. "The Demand for Money: The Development of an Economic Concept." *Journal of Political Economy* 61 (April 1953): 144-159.

Girton, Lance, and Nattress, Dale. "The Monetary Approach to Balance of Payments Analysis: Stocks and Flows and Walras' Law." *Intermountain Economic Review* 8 (Winter 1977): 11-22.

_____, and Roper, Don. "The Evolution of Exchange Rate Policy." Bluford H. Putnam and D. Sykes Wilford, eds. *The Monetary Approach to International Adjustment.* New York: Praeger, 1979. pp. 215-228.

Gordon, Robert J. "Recent Developments in the Theory of Inflation and Unemployment." *Journal of Monetary Economics* 2 (April 1976): 185-219.

Hansen, Alvin H., and Tout, Herbert. "Annual Survey of Business Cycle Theory: Investment and Saving." *Econometrica* 2 (April 1934): 152-167.

Hayek, F. A. "Reflections on the Pure Theory of Money of Dr. J. M. Keynes." *Economica* No. 34 (August 1931): 270-295.

_____. Rejoinder to Mr. Keynes." *Economica* No. 34 (November 1931): 398-403.

Hayek, F. A. "The Place of Menger's Grundsätze in the History of Economic Thought." J. R. Hicks and W. Weber, eds. *Carl Menger and the Austrian School of Economics.* Oxford: The Clarendon Press, 1973, pp. 1-14.

_____. "Three Elucidations of the Ricardo Effect." *Journal of Political Economy* 77 (March/April 1969): 274-285.

Heller, H. R. "The Demand for Money -- the Evidence from the Short-Run Data." *Quarterly Journal of Economics* 79 (May 1965): 291-303.

Hicks, J. R. "Equilibrium and the Trade Cycle." *Economic Inquiry* 18 (October 1980): 523-534.

Hicks, J. R. "A Reconsideration of the Theory of Value, Part I." *Economica*, n.s. 1 (February 1934): 52-76.

_____. "A Suggestion for Simplifying the Theory of Money." *Economica*, n.s. 2 (February 1935): 52-76.

Humphrey, Thomas M. "Monetary Approach to Exchange Rates: The Importance of Dennis H. Robertson." *Commodity Journal* (May 1981): 10-11, 14-16.

_____. "The Monetary Approach to Exchange Rates: Its Historical Evolution and role in Policy Debates." Bluford H. Putnam and D. Sykes Wilford, eds. *The Monetary Approach to International Adjustment*. New York: Praeger, 1979, pp. 134-161.

Hutt, William H. "The Significance of Price Flexibility." Henry Hazlitt, ed. *The Critics of Keynesian Economics*. Princeton: D. Van Nostrand, 1960, pp. 386-403.

Johnson, Harry G. "The Monetary Approach to Balance of Payments: A Non-technical Guide." *Journal of International Economics* 7 (August 1977): 251-268.

_____. "The Monetary Approach to Balance of Payments Theory." *Journal of Financial and Quantitative Analysis* 7 (March 1972): 1555-1572.

Johnson, P. D., and Dierzkowski, H. "The Balance of Payments: An Analytic Exercise." *The Manchester School of Economic and Social Studies* 43 (September 1977): 653-669.

Johnson, W. E. "The Pure Theory of Utility Curves." *Economic Journal* 23 (December 1913): 483-513.

Kaldor, Nicholas, "Capital Intensity and the Trade Cycle." *Economica*, n.s. 6 (May 1939): 127-152.

_____. "Professor Hayek and the Concertina Effect." *Economica*, n.s. 9 (November 1942): 359-283.

Keleher, Robert E. "Of Money and Prices: Some Historical Perspectives." Bluford H. Putnam and D. Sykes Wilford, eds. *The Monetary Approach to International Adjustment*. New York: Praeger, 1979, pp. 19-48.

Keynes, John Maynard. "Review of *Theorie des Geldes und der Umlaufsmittal* by Ludwig von Mises and of *Geld und Kapital* by Friedrick Bendixen." *Economic Journal* 24 (September 1914): 417.

_____. "The Pure Theory of Money: A Reply to Dr. Hayek." *Economica* No. 34 (November 1931): 387-397.

Laidler, David. "Expectations and the Phillips Trade Off: A Commentary." *Scottish Journal of Political Economy* 23 (February 1976): 55-72.

Littlechild, S. C. and Owen, G. "An Austrian Model of the Entrepreneurial Market Process." *Journal of Economic Theory* 23 (December 1980): 361-379.

Lucas, Robert E. "Econometric Policy Evaluation: A Critique." Suppl. to Journal of Monetary Economics, in Karl Brunner and Alan H. Meltzer, eds. *The Phillips Curve and Labor Markets*, Carnegie-Rochester Conference Series on Public Policy, No. 1. New York: North Holland, 1976, pp. 19-46.

"Ludwig von Mises, Distinguished Fellow, 1969." *American Economic Review* 59 (September 1969): Frontispiece.

Machlup, Fritz, "Opening Remarks: Mises, Keynes, and the Question of Influence." Lawrence S. Moss, ed. *The Economics of Ludwig von Mises: Toward a Critical Reappraisal.* Kansas City: Sheed and Ward, 1976, pp. 9-12.

Menger, Carl. "Austrian Marginalism and Mathematical Economics." J. R. Hicks and W. Weber, eds. *Carl Menger and the Austrian School of Economics.* Oxford: The Clarendon Press, 1973, pp. 38-60.

Mises, Ludwig von. "The Balance of Payments and Foreign Exchange Rates." Percy L. Greaves, ed. *On the Manipulation of Money and Credit.* New York: Free Market Books, 1978, pp. 50-55.

_____. "The Economic Aspects of the Pension Problem." Ludwig von Mises. *Planning for Freedom.* 2d enl. ed. Chicago: Libertarian Press, 1962, pp. 83-93.

_____. "Monetary Stabilization and Cyclical Policy." Percy L. Greaves, ed. *On the Manipulation of Money and Credit.* New York: Free Market Books, 1978, pp. 59-117.

_____. "The Stabilization of the Monetary Unit from the Viewpoint of Theory." Percy L. Greaves, ed. *On the Manipulation of Money and Credit.* New York: Free Market Books, 1978, pp. 3-49.

_____. "Wages, Unemployment and Inflation." Ludwig von Mises. *Planning for Freedom.* New York: Libertarian Press, 1962, pp. 150-161.

Moss, Lawrence S. "The Monetary Economics of Ludwig von Mises." Lawrence S. Moss, ed. *The Economics of Ludwig von Mises: Toward a Critical Reappraisal.* Kansas City: Sheed and Ward, 1976, pp. 13-49.

Mussa, Michael. "A Monetary Approach to Balance of Payments Analysis." *Journal of Money, Credit and Banking* 6 (August 1974): 333-351.

Muth, John F. "Rational Expectations and the Theory of Price Movements." *Econometrica* 29 (July 1961): 315-335.

Myhrman, John. "Experiences of Flexible Exchange Rates in Earlier Periods: Theories, Evidence and a New View." *Scandinavian Journal of Economics* 78 (May 1976): 169-196.

Patinkin, Don. "Price Flexibility and Full Employment." *American Economic Review* 38 (September 1948): 543-564. Reprinted with corrections in *Readings In Monetary Theory.* New York: The Blakiston Co., 1951, pp. 252-283.

Phelps, Edmund. "Phillips Curves, Expectations of Inflation, and Optimal Unemployment over Time." *Economica* 34 (August 1967): 254-281.

Phillips, A. W. "The Relation Between Unemployment and the Rate of Change of Money Wage Rates in the United Kingdom, 1861-1957." *Economica* 25 (November 1958): 283-299.

Pigou, A. C. "The Value of Money." *Quarterly Journal of Economics* 32 (November 1917): 38-65.

Roper, Don. "Late Nineteenth Century U.S. Monetary History and the Monetary Theory of an Open Economy." Unpublished manuscript. University of Utah (June 1977).

Rothbard, Murray N. "The Austrian Theory of Money." Edwin G. Dolan, ed. *The*

Foundations of Modern Austrian Economics. Kansas City: Sheed and Ward, 1976, pp. 160-184.

_____. "Praxeology: The Methodology of Austrian Economics." Edwin G. Dolan, Ed. *The Foundations of Modern Austrian Economics*. Kansas City: Sheed and Ward, 1976, pp. 19-39.

Sargent, Thomas, and Wallace, Neil. "Rational Expectations, the Optimal Monetary Instrument, and the Optimal Money Supply Rule." *Journal of Political Economy* 83 (April 1983): 241-254.

Santomero, Anthony, and Seater, John J. "The Inflation-Unemployment Trade-Off: a Critique of the Literature." *Journal of Economic Literature* 16 (June 1978): 499-544.

Sennholz, Hans F. "Postscript." Ludwig von Mises. *Notes and Recollections*. South Holland, Illinois: Libertarian Press, 1978, pp. 145-175.

Stigler, George. "The Development of Utility Theory II." *Journal of Political Economy* 18 (August 1950): 373-396.

Sweezy, Alan R. "The Interpretation of Subjective Value in the Writings of the Austrian Economists." *Review of Economic Studies* 1 (June 1934): 176-185.

Tulloch, Gordon. "Competing Monies." *Journal of Money, Credit and Banking* 7 (November 1975): 491-497.

Whitman, Marina von Nueman. "Global Monetarism and the Monetary Approach to the Balance of Payments." *Brookings Papers on Economic Activity* No. 3 (1975): 491-536.

Wicksell, Knut. "The Influence of the Rate of Interest on Prices." *Economic Journal* 18 (June 1907): 210-221.

Yeager, Leland, "The Methodology of Henry George and Carl Menger." *American Journal of Economics and Sociology* 13 (April 1954): 233-238.

_____. "Toward Understanding Some Paradoxes in Capital Theory." *Economic Inquiry* 14 (September 1976): 313-345.

Zeuthan, F. "Discussion." *Econometrica* 22 (April 1955): 199-200.